DEFENSIVE LIVING

Preserving Your Personal Safety
Through Awareness,
Attitude & Armed Action

SECOND EDITION

ED LOVETTE
DAVE SPAULDING

Foreword by BRUCE SIDDLE

43-08 162nd Street
Flushing, NY 11358
www.LooseleafLaw.com
800-647-5547

First Printing - 2005
Second Printing - 2007
Third Printing - 2009
Fourth Printing - 2010
Fifth Printing - 2012
Sixth Printing - 2013
Seventh Printing - 2014
Eighth Printing - 2015

Library of Congress Cataloging-in-Publication Data

Lovette, Ed, 1944-
Defensive living : preserving your personal safety through awareness, attitude, and armed action / Ed Lovette & Dave Spaulding ; foreword by Bruce Siddle.-- 2nd ed.
p. cm.
Includes index.
ISBN 1-932777-09-1
1. Crime prevention. 2. Self-preservation. 3. Self-protective behavior. 4. Survival skills. 5. Firearms--Use in crime prevention. I. Spaulding, Dave, 1955- II. Title.
HV7431.L69 2005
613.6'6--dc22

2004024597

Cover design by *Sans Serif, Inc.* Saline, Michigan

About the Authors

Mr. Lovette is a retired CIA paramilitary operations officer. He is a former Captain in the U.S. Army Special Forces and is also a ten-year law enforcement veteran, in which capacity he served as a patrol officer, sheriff's deputy and as the senior firearms and tactics instructor for the New Mexico Law Enforcement Academy.

Since retiring, Mr. Lovette has been involved with a variety of programs designed to enhance the security of our U.S. Embassies overseas. He has also been a presenter to police firearms instructors at the annual conferences for the American Society for Law Enforcement Training and for the International Association of Law Enforcement Firearms Instructors. In addition to co-authoring *Defensive Living* with Dave Spaulding, he is the author of *Snubby: The ECQ, Backup and Concealed Carry Standard.* Mr. Lovette currently writes the Survival Savvy column for "Combat Handguns" magazine.

Dave Spaulding retired after 28 years as a lieutenant with the Montgomery County, Ohio, Sheriff's Office in Dayton, Ohio. During his career he has worked in all facets of law enforcement to include communica- tions, corrections, court security, patrol, evidence, investigations, undercover opera- tions and SWAT. A frequent instructor at all of the major police training conferences, he has attended most of the nationally recognized firearms schools. Additionally, he has authored more than 600 articles for various police trade journals and firearms periodicals. He is a member of IALEFI, ASLET, the International Association of Counter-Terrorism and Security Professionals and is the past president of the Ohio Tactical Officers Association. He is also the author of the well-received *Handgun Combatives.* He lives outside Dayton, Ohio, with his wife Diane and their three children.

Ed Lovette
Dave Spaulding

Personal security is a working blend of
awareness, *attitude* and *training* which
allows us to confidently go about
the daily business of living.

Dedications

To Barbara, my bride of 30-some years. Great wife, super mom, world-class grandma. Faithful companion ... my best friend ... my heart...

To our three daughters, Melissa, Melinda and Melanie, who grew up thinking everyone spent their summer vacations in Paulden, Arizona. You have helped us grow from proud parents to proud grandparents...

To my father, Lt. Col. L.E. Lovette, attack pilot, USMC. Veteran of three wars, who taught me how to be survival-minded. An officer and a gentleman... a professional warrior ... the best father a boy could have had ... my personal hero...

To the New Mexico Law Enforcement Academy and the peace officers of the great state of New Mexico, who encouraged me, supported me, and certainly taught me much more than I taught them...

To the dedicated men and women of the Central Intelligence Agency and specifically to the Directorate of Operations, who are, as then-President Reagan said, "...those who serve abroad, often at great personal risk, as the tripwire in America's defense."

To Jeff Cooper, another Marine who has had a tremendous influence on me and who is still the clearest voice in the business today...

To my peers, Massad Ayoob, John Farnam, Evan Marshall and Clint Smith. This is small thanks for always finding time in your busy schedules to share your knowledge and experience with me. You're all a constant reminder that I still have a lot to learn...

To Harry Kane, my editor at *Combat Handguns* and a good personal friend. You kept after me to write until I finally ran out of excuses. Thanks...

And finally, to my good buddy, Lt. Dave Spaulding. A lot of our friends told us that co-authoring a book would be a real test of our friendship. Looking at the finished product, I know my initial decision to seek your help on this project was a sound one. Thanks, partner...

Ed Lovette

To my wife Diane, who stayed at home and raised three wonderful children while I was off trying to find the "answers" to personal survival.

To Amber, Misty and Thomas, the three best children that any father could possibly ask the Lord for.

To Mom and Dad – I hope you are proud.

To my bosses at the Montgomery County Sheriff's Office in Dayton, Ohio. Sheriff Gary Haines, Major Ron Casey, Major Roland Cox (retired) and Major Sam Mains (retired) who allowed me to seek training and knowledge and supported me every step of the way.

To my former SWAT partner, Lt. Dan Pierron (retired). We went through more than a few doors together. Sgt. Jack Yahle and Sgt. Pete Snyder for teaching side-by-side with me through the years.

To Dennis Anderson, Tom Aveni, Massad Ayoob, Mike Beckley, John Benner, Mike Boyle, Bert DuVernay, Sam Faulkner, John Farnam, Bill Groce, Dave Grossi, Ken Hackathorn, Dave Harris, Chuck Humes, Mark Kunnath, Tom Long, Evan Marshall, Dennis Martin, Tom Marx, John Meyer, Vince O'Neill, Scott Ralston, Chuck Remsberg, Larry Scott, John Shaw, Chris Shepperd, Clint Smith, Karl Sokol, Marcus Wynne, John Zamrock and Gene Zink. A cadre of instructors who have deeply impacted my life as well as saving the lives of many, many others.

To Lou Alessi, Dan Donahue, Kim Fiedler, Don Hume, Tony Kanaly, Greg Kramer and Mitch Rosen for making the holsters that save lives.

And finally, to my partner Ed Lovette. Our long distance conversations mean more to me than you will ever know.

Dave Spaulding

Table of Contents

Foreword

by Bruce Siddle

Those of us who study combat performance as a science, recognize that threat recognition and fear management are fundamental principles leading to survival. Both topics always precede any serious training on close quarter combat, firearms training or evasive driving. Yet, the literature on both topics is rare, and what has been written is often esoteric and of little practical value.

This is why I found Ed Lovette and Dave Spaulding's book so refreshing. As a student of the effects of the sympathetic nervous system on combat performance, I study the relationship between survival stress and deteriorating performance, when one is confronted with an "unexpected and spontaneous" deadly force threat. This relationship centers around three common variables in combat; threat recognition, the available time to process the threat, and the time to initiate a survival response. But, the key to survival is "increasing the available time" to select an appropriate response. Here is why:

Man's survival as a species is connected to the Autonomic Nervous System (ANS). This system controls all of the voluntary and involuntary functions of the body, and is divided into parasympathetic and sympathetic systems. The parasympathetic nervous system (PNS) is dominant in non-stress environments where an individual perceives he or she is safe. The PNS controls a number of critical survival functions, such as visual acuity, cognitive processing and fine or complex motor skill execution. However, anytime the brain perceives an imminent deadly force threat, the sympathetic nervous system (SNS) is activated, resulting in an immediate discharge of stress hormones.

The SNS is recognized as the "fight or flight" system. The release of stress hormones by the SNS increases arterial pressure and blood flow to large muscle mass (resulting in enhanced gross motor skill and strength capabilities), vasoconstriction of minor blood vessels at the end of appendages, pupil dilation and cessation of the digestive process.

The combination of these physiological changes helped early man run down his next meal, or avoid becoming a meal for another predator. However, today, survival evolves around fundamental skills such as close quarter combatives, firearms and evasive driving. These skills are based on hand/eye coordination, high levels of acuity or accuracy, and a higher level of cognitive processing. For these skills to work optimally, the PNS must be dominant. Unfortunately, activation of the SNS automatically and uncontrollably inhibits the PNS.

The implication of SNS dominance is sequentially catastrophic to three systems; vision, cognitive processing and fine or complex motor skill performance. The first phase of SNS activation, then, will cause the loss of near vision, disrupt depth perception and collapse the peripheral field by 70%. Now consider that vision is the mother of all senses, and is the primary sensory source on which the brain relies in combat. However, if the visual system is feeding impaired information back to the brain during combat, threat recognition and processing skills will be flawed.

The second phase of survival is cognitive threat processing. This phase starts by identifying a threat from the perceptual senses. Once the threat is identified, the brain searches for the appropriate response, which is then prepared (formatted) in the form of a neural motor program.

Cognitive processing is extremely efficient and lightening fast in non-stress situations (PNS dominance). It is a process, which is normally managed by the cerebral cortex and higher brain functions. But SNS activation inhibits higher brain functions centered in the cerebral cortex, resulting in a deterioration of threat recognition, response selection and ability to communicate complex thoughts. The result is a dramatic increase in survival reaction time.

The final phase of survival is the execution of a motor skill. Typically, survival skills can be segmented into three categories; gross, fine and complex. Almost one hundred years of research has demonstrated that under SNS excitement, only gross motor skills are performed optimally. Fine motor skills such as precision shooting, and complex motor skills like evasive driving, all deteriorate when the SNS is activated.

The SNS research finally helps us understand that success in combat is linked to controlling the SNS. But the key to controlling the SNS lies in understanding that it is primarily activated under two conditions; when we perceive an imminent deadly force threat, and when the time to respond to the threat is minimal. Therefore, a man walking toward us with a knife from a distance of 500 yards will probably not activate the SNS. But being surprised by the same threat from a distance of 10 feet, will almost certainly activate the SNS.

The key to survival is 'increasing the available time' to control the SNS and select an appropriate response.

The gift of this text is the shared research of Dave and Ed. Lt. Dave Spaulding is a police officer who has spent a career studying victims of crimes and learning how to profile what victims did to decrease their survival. Ed Lovette is a retired CIA operations officer who spent the latter part of his career researching, developing and teaching street survival skills for CIA personnel going to high-threat environments. By combining their knowledge, they have identified the process which will give you the skills to see things develop at a distance, increase your time to avoid or evade the threat, and control the SNS.

As a student of survival stress physiology, I have been painfully aware of the lack of literature that focuses on the survival mindset. But when I received the draft of this text, my first response was "finally." For example, Chapter Two examines the basics of scanning for situational awareness. Chapter Three explores the relationship between having a prepared plan and how it will increase your reaction time. Chapter Four targets the process of identifying danger cues, and Chapter Five focuses on the survival mindset. Alone, these four chapters provide us with the insights to control the SNS. But when combined with the final chapters which explore the physical side of survival, this text becomes a stand alone reference to survival.

Introduction

PERSONAL SECURITY IS A WORKING BLEND OF AWARENESS, ATTITUDE AND TRAINING WHICH ALLOWS US TO CONFIDENTLY GO ABOUT THE DAILY BUSINESS OF LIFE AND LIVING.

I was discussing this book the other day with several buddies of mine who had done me the favor of going over a rough draft of it. I explained to them that we wanted to lend a helping hand to the growing number of legally armed private citizens who will be mostly self-educated on personal security matters. The "just plain folks" whose stories you read in the "This Happened to Me" columns in the gun magazines. The courageous citizens whose stories we see all too frequently in our local newspapers and on the nightly news. Most, if not all, of what these individuals learn about protecting themselves and their families, they will learn on their own. They will gain this knowledge from family members, friends, programs put on by their local police and sheriff's departments, their local gun clubs and from life experience. We wanted to provide this group with some good basic information, especially intended for those who were thinking about their own personal security for the first time, and to also pass on some commercially available sources of relevant information that Dave and I had found both beneficial and practical. One of my friends looked thoughtful for a while. When he spoke, he summed up what, in the final analysis, Dave and I would like this book to be. It is the book you would want a family member, or anyone close to you whom you care about, to read if you were concerned about their safety. Because that's who we're writing this for.

Dave and I also agreed that we wanted to keep the emphasis of the book on the individual. As you can see from our definition, we believe that awareness and attitude are the keys to personal security. Training and equipment are useless if you're not "switched on" and willing to do what you have to do. As an example, I have a friend who teaches a modular package he developed for people working in areas with a high terrorist threat. One module deals with situational awareness and attack recognition. The other involves hands-on driver training in evasive maneuvers. This man is the single most knowledgeable individual on terrorist methods of operation and how to avoid them that I know. He has been teaching this program for about a decade with excellent results. He always tells his clients, if they can only afford the time and money to attend one module, they should select the one on situational awareness. Overtime, those students of his who only had this four-hour block of instruction, have performed better during critical incidents than those who opted solely for the driving instruction.

More definitions:

SITUATIONAL AWARENESS IS DEFINED AS A STATE OF GENERAL ALERTNESS WHICH ALLOWS YOU TO TAKE THE ELEMENT OF SURPRISE AWAY FROM THE THREAT.

THE "SURVIVOR'S ATTITUDE" IS THE WILLINGNESS TO DO WHAT YOU HAVE TO DO; REFUSING IN ADVANCE TO BECOME A VICTIM; NEVER, EVER, GIVING UP.

THREAT MANAGEMENT TRAINING FOCUSES ON THOSE SKILLS WHICH GIVE A LONE INDIVIDUAL THE HIGHEST CHANCE OF SUCCESS TO AVOID, EVADE OR COUNTER AND SAFELY ESCAPE FROM A CRIMINAL ASSAULT ON THE STREET, IN THE VEHICLE AND IN THE HOME.

During one of the infrequent times Dave and I actually got to sit down together and discuss the writing of this book, Barbara, my bride of thirty-some years, joined us as we kicked around the title. Finally she said, "Why don't you guys call it something like 'Living Defensively?' " This with the air of finality of a grandmother who was almost forced to shoot a rock-wielding rioter once-upon-a-time. Her only thought as he approached the car was should she roll the window down or just shoot through the glass. I suspect what saved his life at the last moment was the sudden realization that he was on the receiving end of "The Look," that awesome weapon of mass destruction unique to the female of the species. Dave and I agreed rapidly and in unison that hers was a most excellent suggestion.

To put it simply, then, we are going to share with you here a street-proven methodology designed to respond to those situations in which your attacker(s) has "the ability and the opportunity to place you and/or yours in jeopardy." We are going to look at how you can take advantage of your strongest personal security weapons, Awareness, Attitude and Training in order to Detect-Assess-Avoid-Evade-Counter and Safely Escape from those who would do you harm.

Since *Defensive Living* was first published we have suffered the unthinkable, a major terrorist attack on U.S. soil. As a result of that attack we have declared war on the terrorists. As I write this in October of 2004 there is a terrorist threat advisory warning of the possibility of yet another attack in America prior to the November presidential elections. The intelligence suggests that something might happen but what might happen, where it will happen, when it will happen and who the bad guys are, are all questions with no answers.

This is where you come in. In the chapter entitled "What Can I Do?" I'll explain in detail why "Uncle Sam Needs You." The short version is that terrorist activities are very tough to conduct in a country where the citizens pay attention to what is going on around them and quickly report suspicious activities to the local authorities.

And finally, it will be quickly apparent to the reader that while Dave's and my name appear on the cover of this book, a lot of other people actually wrote it. Thank you is inadequate. Sometimes the only way you can repay a debt of gratitude is by passing on that which was given to you. We are hopeful that our many "coauthors" will therefore appreciate the true measure of our respect for all that they have given to us.

Chapter 1

Is Your Mind Putting Your Body at Risk?

When Dave and I outlined the chapters for this book, I suggested that we needed to open with a security survey. That way the reader could either start to develop or reinforce his or her own security plan from the outset. Dave let me get to about reason number eight as to why I thought we should do things this way. At which point he asked me if I really wanted to do a full-blown security survey or something more along the lines of a personal risk assessment. That stopped me. The more I thought about it the more I realized he was exactly right. It's easy to see why his department made him a lieutenant and I never got past patrolman.

A risk assessment is your personal threat assessment superimposed over your personal lifestyle survey. Threat assessment is exactly what it says. Do you have a specific problem, such as a stalker, or are you concerned about the welfare of your family? We can certainly all make the case that we are generally at risk from random violence. Just pick up your local newspaper or watch the nightly news. The lifestyle survey is how and where you and your family live, work, play and travel.

What we really want you to do is to take a look at yourself with the intention of raising your security consciousness, heightening your personal awareness. While deadbolts, good lighting and where you park your car are considerations, the only part of the process you always have control over is you. You can spend a lot of your earnings on making your home a fortress, but what do you do if you're a college student living in a dorm. Or your job requires frequent travel and you spend a lot of time in motels. Maybe your job requires you to work late at night or you must drive through a rough section of town to get there. Perhaps your sister thinks that she is being stalked by her ex-boyfriend and she wants you to spend a few days with her.

When you start to assess your personal security risk, it is helpful to begin with what you know about yourself. Do you unknowingly do things which draw attention to yourself or that make you vulnerable? Do you give off signals that make the predators salivate? Do you provide the opportunity for a crime of opportunity? Don't be surprised if your answer to all the above is, "I don't know."

I frequently encountered this response during the time I was an instructor for my agency's personal security training programs which our officers attended in preparation for their overseas assignments. In the classroom everyone would nod "yes" when asked if they understood what we were talking about. They filled in the blanks correctly on the test. But there were always several students in each class who couldn't pass the simplest of the street awareness practical exercises. They would come away from the training frustrated and I would come away confused. Quite by accident I got the first glimpse into what might be contributing to their/my dilemma while reading a book published by the Institute for the Study of Diplomacy entitled, *Overseas Security: Our People are the Key*. A study in the book notes that certain personality types are what the Meyers-Briggs psychological test describes as "conceptualizers." "Conceptualizers by nature have trouble noticing such details as whether they're under surveillance or whether there's something unusual about their houses when they go home at night." Bingo!

After a little trial-and-error we found a way to help those students achieve better results in class. Obviously, what we wanted for them was a positive learning experience which would facilitate their long-term retention of the necessary skills. At the beginning of the awareness sessions we would discuss the fact that some people have trouble concentrating on details and then we'd ask the class a few simple questions. "Does your spouse constantly remind you that you never notice anything?" "Have you ever arrived at work only to suddenly realize that you don't remember large parts of the drive?" "Do you not remember because you were daydreaming or maybe mentally drawing up the blueprint for the new addition for your home?" This helped the student identify a specific problem area he or she would have to work on a little harder to overcome. As Clint Smith, Director of Thunder Ranch, tells his classes, "This don't make it bad. It just makes it real."

(We'd early on decided against asking for a show of hands since it would have included too many of the instructors!)

At about the same time we discovered this we started some group exercises designed to address a separate issue. Quite by accident we found out that our "conceptualizers" caught on much quicker when they saw through the eyes of others. So we all learned that some people have natural inhibitors which work against their awareness of what is going on around them. But unless someone talks to them about this possibility and how to deal with it they will continue to nod "yes" when appropriate, fill in the right blanks and flunk *Street Awareness 101*. To simply tell these folks to be aware of their immediate environment is not good enough. You must also show them how.

> *Several of the ladies in the office decided to have a dinner party featuring popular local dishes. The recipes for this meal required a visit to a market in a less than desirable section of town so one Saturday morning, counting on strength in numbers, three of them made the trip. During their stroll through the market they often had to walk in single file due to the crowds. Spices in hand, they returned to the home of one of the secretaries at which time she discovered that her money was gone. Someone had sliced through the left front pocket of her jeans and extracted her cash.*

When I talked with her about the incident, she could remember nothing unusual during their time at the market except that at one point they had walked through a cloud of some sort of dust. As she described this to me she raised both hands and animatedly fanned an imaginary dust cloud away from her face. (This was a common tactic employed by pickpockets in South America. The dust, shaving cream or water was used to distract both the attention and the hands of their intended target). How come they picked this particular woman of the three? How long had they watched these women to learn where they carried their money? (None of them were carrying purses). As we continued talking, she told me that something like this had happened to her on every one of her overseas assignments. It also became painfully apparent during our conversation that she was oblivious to what went on around her.

So these ladies knew they were going into a seedy part of town and elected to go as a group. They went during the day and left their purses at home. While they'd all had previous overseas assignments in high crime cities, none of them saw anyone who might have been interested in the three. But in that sea of humanity swam a predator who, like the great white shark, located his prey, identified the weakest member of the group, and in broad daylight separated her from her money, undetected.

As an inveterate people-watcher I am constantly amused and amazed. The other day I was sitting in a hotel lobby waiting for some friends I was supposed to meet. From where I sat I could watch the parking lot in front of the hotel. Pretty soon an attractive middle-aged woman pulled up. As she opened the car door to get out, I noticed that she tossed something onto the pavement. She fussed around in the car with the door open for some time before stepping out of the car. There was still snow on the ground so you can imagine my surprise on seeing that this well-dressed lady was bare footed. What I'd seen her throw out of the car were her shoes. She took her own sweet time getting them on. You tell me. How vulnerable was she and for how long? How many times had she done this in the very same spot? Amazing how the simplest of habits can set us up. How well can you run or fight bare footed?

So because we're human and because of the way our minds work, we can unknowingly, unthinkingly raise our risk profile. To counter this we must not lose sight of the fact that most street crimes are crimes of opportunity. You can provide this opportunity by appearing to be an easy target. The way you walk; if you appear distracted, uncertain, aimless, confused; your age, sex and physical condition. One study claims that it takes a predator about seven seconds to assess you as prey. And the actual attack will happen very quickly and in some cases will be unspeakably brutal.

Which brings us to our next point. Gratuitous violence that catches us unawares can be stunning. That's why some people freeze during an attack. Fight or flight never become considerations. The majority of my students in recent years have never even been in a schoolyard fistfight. However, since childhood they may have witnessed thousands of violent acts delivered to them with the sterile packaging of supermarket chicken courtesy of television and movies. It is not real. It does not touch them. Through no fault of their own, violence is at best an intellectual concept. It is something that only happens to others. This presents an enormous challenge to them during personal security training because they often have no frame of reference for what the instructor is saying. They hear the explanations for why they should or should not do something. They are able to perform the indicated exercise to the appropriate level during the training. But they may not take very much of what they learn with them when they complete the training if the instructor hasn't done his homework.

Contrast this with their potential attacker. Unlike them, he is no stranger to physical violence. He has no conscience and no remorse, hence no hesitation. He does not fear the police or the courts. He is probably younger and physically stronger than you. Chances are good that he is under the influence of alcohol and/or narcotics. He already has a plan. Are you mentally prepared to face this individual and use whatever level of force, up to and including lethal force, which may be required to stop him?

The driver sat paralyzed behind the wheel of her new car and watched as the gunman, armed with an AK-47, walked toward her. He stopped at the driver's window and stared at her for a moment, then turned and shot the male driver of the car in the lane next to her. As the gunman stood with his back to her firing into the car she could have reached out and touched him. All this time her mind, refusing to accept what she was seeing, kept repeating over and over, "I hope he doesn't scratch the finish on my new car."

The gunman continued walking between the lines of cars shooting only males, sparing the women. A high-ranking political official drove by the scene and remarked to his driver that it looked like someone was making a movie. Also in the double lane of traffic stopped at the light was an intelligence officer who had recently returned to the U.S. from a lengthy overseas tour. During this assignment he had been actively targeted by a terrorist organization which claimed responsibility for the deaths of three Americans. He had the heater turned up against the deep winter cold of late January and was listening to his favorite radio station. An eruption of glass fragments caught his eye as the AK rounds chewed through the windshield of a vehicle several car lengths ahead of his. From his position he could neither see the gunman nor hear the gunfire but habits fireformed into his psyche by four years of living under the gun took over. Quickly he turned the radio off and was starting to roll the window down when he heard the AK. Without hesitation he cranked the steering wheel hard to the left, mashed the accelerator and fishtailed across the frozen median in a giant U-turn. The tires picked up traction as they grabbed the pavement and he sped away from the scene.

A fourth individual, who had recently completed his certification as a volunteer paramedic, also saw the flying glass and instantly thought, "Christ, there's been an accident!" By the time he'd grabbed his trauma kit and run up to the lead vehicle the gunman had jumped into a waiting car and fled.

Same incident. Four different people. Four totally different reactions. Each saw approximately the same scene and processed what they were seeing and hearing based on their level of involvement, training, background and life experiences.

We'll conclude this chapter the same way we started. Only by now, hopefully, you have a better understanding of the point we're trying to make when we say that personal security starts with you and what you know about yourself. Is your mind putting your body at risk?

Chapter 2

Increasing Your Awareness

The woman was not sure whether to be concerned or to admit to herself that she was over-reacting because of the class. The wife of a senior U.S. military officer stationed in Europe, a few days earlier she and her husband had attended a briefing on the growing terrorist threat in their area which reviewed several recent incidents and some precautions they should take. The young man had been standing on the street corner across from the house for about an hour as if he were waiting for someone. From time to time he would walk up and down the street. "Probably trying to stay warm," she thought to herself. The evening chill set in quickly as the sun dropped below the mountains behind her house.

She busied herself with supper checking the window from time to time to see if he was still there. Just as she was about to turn back to putting the finishing touches on the salad a car pulled up alongside the young man. Without getting out of the car the driver of the vehicle handed the man a jacket and drove away. She noted the license number and, telling herself not to panic, shakily dialed her husband's work number. No answer. Car phone. No answer. She had just pushed the "redial" button when she heard the sound of the iron gate as it slid open. He always drove himself home, refusing the driver his rank entitled him to. He'd get out of the car, open the gate, drive the car into the big driveway in front of the house, then get out of the car again to close the gate. She grabbed his arm, told him to forget the car and hurried him into the house with her. She told him what she'd seen and he immediately called base security. The arrest of the young man and the license number she'd hastily copied provided officials with the necessary information to begin an investigation that ultimately disrupted a terrorist operation which planned to kidnap the senior officer.

As we said in the first chapter, simply telling someone to be alert, be aware is not sufficient. ("Be alert. Why? Because the country is looking for a few good lerts.") Excuse me? So let's take a look at some things we can do to heighten our awareness. Mental awareness is the end result, the third step, of a three-step process. Failure to do steps one and two explains why a lot of folks never get very good at step three. The first step is mental preparation, perhaps best described as some bridges you need to cross. These are the stretching exercises for step two. The second step, mental conditioning, is an ongoing process which helps you get into shape and stay in shape from the neck up.

First, mental preparation. This is part of your commitment to personal security. A self-test which requires you to deal with some critical issues before the battle, not during it. It helps you put these issues in perspective even if your honest answer is, "I'm not sure, but I think so." Consider then:

1) Doing a reality check. Getting your head out of the sand. This is an acceptance of the fact that we live in an increasingly violent world and that one day we might be confronted by this violence. That's the bad news. The good news is we can do something about it.

2) Doing an attitude check. The defeatist attitude is a self-fulfilling prophecy. It is most often identified by the phrase, "If they want me, they're gonna' get me." If you honestly believe that, close this book and pass it on to someone else. We can't help you. More to the point, you can't help yourself.

3) Making an agreement with yourself that when (not if) your day comes, you will not give UP. Even if you have to give IN.

4) Asking yourself if you're ready for the responsibility that comes with having a firearm for self-defense.

He was an agent for the U.S. Drug Enforcement Administration who had been temporarily assigned to one of his agency's offices abroad. He was doing some last minute shopping before catching a flight home the next day. He had hailed a cab, got in and sat down on the back seat and closed the door when the driver of the cab turned around and stuck a gun in his face and demanded money. The agent was wearing a pair of handmade elephant hide boots which he had just picked up. He had his Glock 19 stuffed in one boot and a large sum of cash stashed in the other. He reached for neither. He had learned a long time ago to carry a little money, mostly small bills, separate from the bulk of his cash. Reaching into his shirt pocket, he handed the driver this "chump change," telling him in the local language that was all he had. As he was talking, the agent opened the cab door. He stepped out and walked away. His agency commended his level-headed response to this incident.

Mental conditioning, as the term implies, helps you develop your awareness skills and then keep them sharp. In my studies of the subject I have found two people who take a very common sense user-friendly approach to helping you both understand what mental conditioning is and how best to practice it. The first is Jeff Cooper, the father of modern pistolcraft. There's no sense in me trying to explain what Jeff Cooper has already said best. I especially like the simplicity of his two part approach. One part is called the "What if?" exercise. The other is "X's and O's," a practical exercise. We'll come back to him in a minute.

More recently, in preparation for this book in fact, I read an excellent presentation on the subject in an article Marcus Wynne did for *Combat Handguns*, entitled, "Living in Condition Yellow." Marcus is a private consultant who has done an enormous amount of research into how to improve your performance under stress. His thoughts on mental conditioning dovetail nicely with Cooper's. I especially like them because they include the other senses in addition to vision and his "five minutes a day" approach should prove comfortable to anyone who is seeing this for the first time. It is also a good warmup for the "X's and O's."

Cooper: "What if?" poses a tactical problem you must resolve. Unfortunately, your local newspapers and the nightly TV news are usually chock full of all sorts of horrible things that have happened during the day. Just ask yourself how you would have handled these situations. Could they have been avoided? If not, what options could you have used to evade or counter and safely extract yourself from the incident. Movies are another good source of situations. While they tend to stretch your imagination somewhat, you can count on the hero to do everything wrong, at least from a real-world perspective. And you will see some truly awful technique and absolutely frightful gun handling, guaranteed.

Wynne: "We need to get out of our own way and relearn trust in that intuitive processing. We need to pay attention to it . . . We can consciously train this ability, five minutes at a time, by asking ourselves, 'What am I seeing around me right now?' and enumerating the trees, people, cars that are in our visual field. 'What am I hearing right now?' and carefully listening to the birds, the voices of the people walking by, the planes passing overhead, the sound of car doors slamming. By asking, 'What am I feeling right now?' and noticing the twinges in our stomach, the tightness in our shoulders, the tension in our foreheads. By asking, 'What do I know right now?' and paying attention to the messages we get from the sixth sense of intuition. We can learn to do this, before we need to use it, by practicing situational awareness in five minute blocks throughout the day."

Cooper: The "X's and O's" is a street awareness test. In Cooper's *Principles of Personal Defense* he describes it as follows: "Make it a game. Keep a chart. Every time anyone is able to approach you from behind without your knowledge, mark down an X. Every time you see anyone you know before he sees you, mark down an O. Keep the O's in front of the X's. A month with no X's establishes the formation of correct habits."

Mental preparation + Mental conditioning = Mental awareness. In the introduction we defined mental (situational) awareness as a state of general alertness which allows you to take the element of surprise away from the threat. Many of you will recognize this as Cooper's definition of Condition Yellow. (We'll discuss the Color Code in the next chapter). Awareness has also been described as being totally conscious of your immediate environment.

While we're on definitions, for reasons which we'll go into in the next few lines, we consider your immediate environment to be 21'/360°. This is your ideal personal safety zone, whether you are on foot, in a car, or seated in a public place. Obviously, as soon as you get into an elevator or ride the subway this area shrinks. Pedestrian traffic in a big city may also make these limits seem overly ambitious. But as we get into WHAT to look for you'll see examples of how to pick people out of a crowd whose actions are out of place. They don't fit into the picture. Their movement patterns disrupt the rhythm of the street.

There are two reasons for the 21' safety zone. One is reaction time, which we'll discuss in detail in a subsequent chapter. The other is what may be called "critical distance." For now consider, as an example which nearly everyone has heard of, the "21 foot" rule in dealing with edged weapons. This is the lasting contribution to armed encounters provided by Lt. Dennis Tueller of the Salt Lake City Police Department. It is based on the action vs. reaction principle. An individual who threatens you with an edged weapon can cover 21 feet in 1.5 seconds or less. Just about the time it takes you to draw and fire one hastily aimed shot. Here we must also take into account that it is not easy to stop a determined assailant instantly with accurate handgun fire, even with multiple hits; and that a person shot squarely through the heart can continue to fight for ten to fifteen seconds. Thus if you are threatened by an individual armed with an edged weapon, you may appropriately defend yourself at seven yards rather than waiting until he is within arm's length. Reducing our defensive space to less than seven yards drastically reduces our reaction time in worst case scenarios.

Critical distance is 21' to contact. Most of the types of violent encounters (critical incidents) we discuss in this book take place within this distance. Most police officers are killed within this distance. You may hear it referred to as the "danger zone" or "the hole." We have learned from John Farnam of Defense Training

International that beyond seven yards your chances of surviving an armed confrontation go up dramatically.

The 360° requirement reminds us that we humans are most vulnerable from behind. Not being able to see to the rear is a chink in our natural defenses. So where we sit, how we stand, how we use shadows and reflections, how we use our hearing, constantly scanning our rearview mirrors when we're in a vehicle- all must be employed to protect our back.

We'll end this chapter with something for you to consider. There is a lot of good personal security info available to us today. To be honest, I'm a little overwhelmed by it, especially the checklists of what to do for each specific type of problem. I'm always afraid I'll get the rules for elevator behavior confused with what I'm supposed to do at the ATM. For me it is easier (for which read about all I can handle) to concentrate on increasing my awareness, being especially attuned to everything going on in my little 21'/360° safety bubble, and using large doses of common sense.

If personal weapons are part of your defensive plan, a quality handgun, a holster for same, a folding knife and a small flashlight are a good start. Shown here is the Heckler and Koch USP Compact in .40 caliber, an Alessi CQC belt holster, a Masters of Defense "Keating" folding knife and a Sure Fire 3P combat light.

Chapter 3

Cooper's Color Code

The purpose of increasing our awareness is, best case, to see the problem before the problem sees us or, second best, at least at about the same time. The sooner we see the problem the more time we have. (Time that may be measured in heartbeats so we cannot afford to waste it.) The more time we have the more options we have. The more options we have the better we are able to develop a plan (albeit a hasty one!) which will give us the best chance for achieving the desired outcome of choice, i.e., confrontation avoidance. Seeing the problem too late = less time = fewer options = incomplete/no plan = high chance of a less than desirable outcome. As long as we are reacting to whatever the bad guy chooses to do to us we are not in charge of the situation. We are responding defensively. And the longer we are on the defensive the harder it becomes to achieve tactical dominance of the situation. Not good.

So anything that allows us to buy time gives us an edge. If we use this time to select our response before the games begin, we can possibly turn them off (avoid). If forced to respond we can react quicker, more aggressively, more decisively (evade, counter). Our mind naturally goes through various levels of alert/alarm when confronted by anything it perceives as a threat. If we know this and understand how it affects us both mentally and physically we can make it work to our advantage. (We'll deal with this in detail in the chapter on Survival Stress and the Conditioned Response).

Kudos again must go to Jeff Cooper who recognized the importance of controlling this process and devised what he calls the "Color Code" to deal with it. The Color Code has been in continuous use now for the last two decades. It may well be the best example we have of a simple solution to a complex problem. In his book *Fireworks* Cooper explained the Color Code thusly:

I have devised a simple color code which is used to enable the student to assume a state of mind appropriate to the various stages of readiness he may need. A man cannot live constantly looking down his sights with his finger on the trigger . . . BUT YOU CAN, WITH A BIT OF PRACTICE, LEARN TO SWITCH YOUR MIND INTO A MORE ADVANCED STATE OF READINESS, IN WHICH CERTAIN PRESET DECISIONS ARE EASIER TO MAKE. You do this naturally, but usually by means of an infinitely variable gradation. The Color Code makes it easier, by means of definite, pre-considered steps.

He defines them as follows:

1) Condition White- a normal non-combative state of mind
2) Condition Yellow- a state of relaxed alertness
3) Condition Orange- state of alarm
4) Condition Red- defensive combat

While these definitions are still fresh in your mind let's amplify them a bit. There is probably a fancy name for these but I call them mental pegs. They help you decide which rung of the alertness ladder you need to be on, as one friend of mine puts it. Condition White is the state of mind of the victim. Totally UNconscious of their immediate environment. Cooper reminds us that we go into Condition Yellow (GENERALLY conscious of your immediate environment) any time we strap on our sidearm. Anytime you leave your comfort zone, i.e., you may go from a known environment to an unknown environment (home to street), or from a known situation to an unknown situation (you're watching TV and someone knocks at the front door), you should go into Condition Yellow. Any time you pick up a firearm to defend yourself, to check out that strange noise in the kitchen, anytime you see two or more of the danger signs, you should be in Condition Orange (SPECIFICALLY conscious of your immediate environment). Condition Red is where you need to be during any armed confrontation in progress. This includes the full range of possibilities. Shots may have been exchanged and/or you are holding the subject at gunpoint.

If you buy into the Color Code, once you've internalized it, you can forget about trying to memorize the usual lists you often see on things to do to avoid becoming a victim. Your common sense and your awareness will do this for you. Never again will you casually answer the doorbell in your home. You will automatically pay more attention to where you sit in a restaurant, how you check out that strange noise downstairs, why the dogs are barking, whose footsteps those are behind you in the parking garage, who's around you at the ATM. The Detect-Assess phase if you will. But how does it work for us in those instances when the use of force is unavoidable. When we must Counter.

It will work as well as we let it. Actually Cooper designed the Color Code to assist you when you must react under the effects of survival stress. The trick is you must practice it under those conditions. If you do not learn the application of the technique in scenarios designed to induce survival stress, it will not be there for you when you need it. For example, as Cooper explains it, people in a high state of readiness (Condition Red) will fire at noise or movement UNLESS PROPERLY PROGRAMMED. In Condition Red, then, you MUST PROGRAM ON SOMETHING SPECIFIC BEFORE YOU REACT. This is why training on managing potentially lethal confrontations places such heavy emphasis on controlling and watching the hands. Failing to do this is why police officers shoot each other during building searches or one family member shoots another mistaking them for a burglar. Time and again I've watched students during a scenario shoot then immediately wince, shake their head and mutter something unprintable. Their trigger finger got ahead of the signal their eyes were sending to the brain. Afterwards they would usually say that even as they were pulling the trigger they knew they shouldn't be. Once they let the process work and got confidence in their ability to use it the results were phenomenal. They could tell you not only that the "assailant" had a beer can in his hand but what brand it was!

> *As often happens, what had started out as a routine arrest turned into a hostage situation. The subject, armed with a lock blade folding knife, was holed up in a motel room with his girlfriend. Every few minutes he would come to the door and talk to the negotiator while holding the knife at the girl's throat. The tactical team had decided to grab the girl the next time he came to the door. The plan was for one officer to grab her and pivot away from the doorway leaving a clear shot, if one presented itself. The officer knelt beside the door for what seemed like hours and then it slowly opened. He had to wait until the girl took one more step and then he moved. What they hadn't counted on was the speed of her boyfriend, the hostage-taker. As the officer pivoted away from the door with one arm around the girl's waist, the boyfriend instantly launched himself at the officer's exposed back and began to repeatedly stab him with forceful "icepick" style blows. He stabbed the officer at least three times before being shot. Frantic officers quickly checked their brother officer to see if the knife had penetrated the body armor he was wearing. The armor was not scratched. They could find no knife marks anywhere. For that matter, they couldn't find the knife either. A search subsequently located it behind the motel. The boyfriend had thrown it out of the bathroom window before he came to the door the last time.*

This incident took place about 20 years ago. The available lighting was good. The stopping shot was fired with a shotgun from about 15 feet. As armchair quarterbacks it is easy to ask how this could happen. It is probably a better bet to assume that there but for the grace of God go I when you consider the dynamics. The suspect had been seen several times with a knife at his girlfriend's throat. The situation drags on for hours. The plan to resolve the incident is gutsy and depends on split-second timing on the part of the rescuing officer and the officer covering him with the shotgun. In this compressed time frame when the subject strikes the officer he does so in a manner consistent with someone holding a knife. The officers on this tactical team had never heard of the Color Code. A coroner's jury ruled the shooting justifiable. How do you think the courts would rule today in your area? WHAT IF we used a little imagination to come up with a scenario using pieces of this incident which turned it into a problem which suddenly confronts a private citizen who is legally armed . . .

Clint Smith, who must be at least as quotable as Will Rogers, sums this chapter up best. He tells his students, in his best Marine Corps Drill Instructor's voice, "Get the best training you can afford. But train with the understanding that most firearm's practice is about 75% physical and 25% mental. A gunfight is about 75% mental and about 25% physical."

Chapter 4

Danger Signs

Up to this point we've talked about the importance of being aware, alert, "tuned in." What we need to address now are those things specifically that we should be aware of, alert for, "tuned in" to. In the interest of simplicity we are going to call these danger signs, a generic name for anything that warns us we may have a problem. Danger signs are cues that may be subtle (easy to miss) or not so subtle (impossible to ignore). They are most often visual but may include the other senses as well. Different threats have different cues. A woman walking to her car in the parking lot of a shopping mall, an officer making a vehicle stop and a businessman concerned about the possibility of a terrorist kidnapping are all looking for different danger signs. Those that we will deal within this chapter will be the obvious ones most often encountered by victims of street crimes. They will be visual, auditory, intuitive and situational.

Visual indicators are what the woman walking to her car in the parking lot of the shopping mall is looking for. We have extracted them from two different sources. The first is *Surviving in the Age of Fear*. I consider this book to be the premier text on street crime awareness. The author, Bill Langlois, was mugged 256 times as a decoy for the San Francisco Police Department's street crime unit. The second source is the Sexual Harassment Assault Rape Prevention training program designed by Bruce Siddle. Siddle is the Executive Director of PPCT Management Systems, Inc. He is the foremost researcher in the field today on the design of training systems that permit an officer to perform at his highest potential while under the stress induced by a lethal confrontation.

These are the danger signs Langlois identified as the ones he was most likely to see just prior to being mugged:

1) Excessive or prolonged eye contact. An oldie but a goodie. The bad guys will tell you that the only people who will look you in the eye on the street are other bad guys or cops. There is at least one documented case in which members of a hit team were trained to avoid this natural predatory response. They concentrated on developing their vision by reading newspapers held several feet from the side of their head. They never looked directly at their intended victim until they were right on top of him and drawing their weapon. People trained in this technique develop a curious stilted gait because they are trying to keep their head movement to a minimum in order to see better. This manner of walking is very easy to spot once you've seen it. So, in essence, they trade one danger sign for another.

2) People who appear to approach you deliberately. This is one of the fastest ways to spot problems in crowds. Everybody is going with the flow but this guy.

3) People who move (with you) when you do.

4) Predatory movements. Circling, splitting up, trying to get behind you.

5) Distractions. This may be verbal. "Gotta light?" Or it may be physical as in someone bumping into you.

Siddle has studied danger signs extensively as part of his continuing research into stimulus-based responses which can enhance performance during critical incidents. His observations closely parallel those of Langlois:

1) He (the predator) will establish ideal hunting grounds and find a casual-looking surveillance point.

2) He will begin following you if you are in a public environment to ascertain whether you would be an easy target. He's already determined that you're vulnerable. He is following you to find location and opportunity. (see 5 below)

3) An assailant will follow you by matching your walking speed.

4) Before he makes contact, he will look around for witnesses.

5) He will look for a point to ambush you with low visibility to avoid unexpected witnesses.

6) Immediately before the attack, he will quickly enter your personal safe zone.

Auditory danger signs are probably the second most common type of cue. Shouts, verbal threats, footsteps, heavy breathing, someone trying to force entry into your home are all examples of auditory danger signs. Probably the worst case I have of this is one in which a couple, unarmed, decided to investigate the sounds of someone downstairs at about 2:00 A.M.. In the kitchen they encountered three individuals armed with AK-47's. They held the husband at gunpoint while taking turns with his wife.

On a more upbeat note, one of my favorite examples came from a crusty old New York police sergeant, now retired. He was explaining to me how he and his partner spotted armed individuals. How people (who are carrying a concealed handgun) walk, how they react to the presence of a police officer, and how they pat or tug at their clothing are some of the indicators street crime units nationwide use in high crime areas to get unauthorized firearms and their users off the street. He said that they took hundreds of guns off the street each year and thought they knew all of the telltale signs. In his thick Brooklyn accent he continued, "Just goes to show you that Murphy has a sense of humor. My partner and I were sitting in a booth in a small diner eating, when a man came in and sat down in the booth in front of ours. As he did so we heard the unmistakable 'clunk' the concealed handgun made as it banged into the back of the wooden booth. Easiest gun collar we ever made," he chuckled.

Intuitive danger signs have to do with what we often refer to as the "sixth sense." Police officers learn early-on to trust these feelings. "I knew the guy was dirty before he ever opened his mouth." We may say to ourselves, "Something doesn't feel right about this," or "What's wrong with this picture?" Gavin De Becker describes intuition as "knowing without knowing why" in his book, *The Gift of Fear*. This book is probably the most practical and useful treatment of the subject of the role of intuition in personal protection available today. The first seven chapters of the book alone make it worth the price. "Trust your instincts." "Go with your gut." We've heard it so often we may fail to treat such advice seriously. But De Becker reminds us "that intuition heeded is far more valuable than simple knowledge."

> *The woman was shopping in a mall near her home when she thought she heard her name announced on the public address system. Sure enough, there it was. "Would the owner of the blue Honda Accord bearing Florida license number ABC-123 please report to the parking lot? Your vehicle has been involved in an accident." Something she could not define made her suspicious. She found a security guard and asked him to verify the message for her. It turned out to be a hoax.*

Situational danger signs are best described by the popular phrase, "You don't want to go there." You are pushed into a car, the person forces his way into your home, they want you to lie down on the floor, they want to tie you up, gag and blindfold you, they want to search you (and you're carrying a concealed weapon). In incident after incident these actions have proven themselves as reliable indicators that the situation is about to become violent. A decision has been made for you. If you can't run, this may be the only chance you will have to, literally, fight for your life.

Chapter 5

The Use of Force Continuum

It is easy to distinguish those who understand this concept from those who don't. The ones who don't are the same folks that bring a knife to a gunfight. The use of force continuum is a scale which graphically shows what your response options are depending on the level of threat which confronts you. It is the "How to" of Avoid - Evade - Counter. It will encourage you to bring a gun to a knife fight. As a simple analogy, if we consider the gun a tool which can lawfully be used when we are threatened with lethal violence, then we need some other tools which we can use when the situation requires a less-than-lethal response. If we can only talk to our assailant or shoot him our tool box may charitably be said to be inadequate. We need to understand that the progression of the force continuum is much like that of a confrontation. The incident may start with words and escalate into a fist fight. The situation may erupt so quickly that there is no time to consider other options (or they are inappropriate) and we are forced to immediately resort to deadly force. We need to be able to articulate this to our attorney. The force continuum helps guide us through this process.

So on one end of the scale you have the limited no-contact responses (presence, eye contact, verbal warnings). In the middle are the less-than lethal options. I found an excellent explanation of when these tools are to be used in a publication entitled *The Pepper Spray Evaluation Project* which we will discuss in detail shortly. The report states that you are justified in using less-than-lethal force, "if verbal commands are ineffective or inappropriate, and you reasonably believe you will become engaged in a fight, i.e., the subject is moving toward you and you reasonably perceive, based on the individual's demeanor and/or words, that he is going to engage you in a fight."

And on the other end is lethal force, which can only be used under very specific circumstances. Massad Ayoob tells his

LFI students that you can legally use deadly force to defend yourself only when you are in "imminent and OTHERWISE UNAVOIDABLE danger of death or serious bodily harm." Thus if you can avoid the use of lethal force or the situation does not warrant its use, you need some other options (tools).

There are two schools of thought on how many tools you really need. One is "the more the merrier." The other is that "less is best." Siddle's research indicates that the fewer responses you have for a specific threat, the quicker you can respond. And the simpler these threat-specific response options are the more likely they are to work for you when the chips are down. Ideally, you should have a tool for each level of difficulty, but that is probably impractical for many of us. Let's take a look at the force continuum and then you can decide for yourself what tools you need.

1) Presence
2) Leave
3) Eye contact
4) Verbal warnings
5) Unarmed countermeasures
6) Oleoresin capsicum
7) Impact weapons
8) Firearms or vehicle

Presence: This generally refers to uniformed police whose mere presence is often enough to discourage trouble. However, YOUR presence may be enough to change the balance of power in the eyes of a predator.

Leave: The military calls this a strategic withdrawal. We might refer to it as "putting our knees in the breeze." The best evaluation I ever heard of this option was how would you rather be remembered? "Old Evan sure can run when he puts his mind to it" or "He certainly looks natural lying there like that."

Eye contact: Once you make eye contact you have also made a statement. "They" are no longer invisible. You are aware of them. And you are ready for them. They are just about to "make your day." In some circumstances this may be known as "walking tall when you're feeling small." But they don't know that!

Verbal warnings: Coupled with eye contact this can be a powerful dissuader. It is startling. It attracts unwanted attention. It puts you in charge. But you need to practice what you're going to say in role play scenarios. It is very difficult for some folks to talk "at volume" to another human being. The best example I have is a bad joke. The one about the nervous robber holding up his first "Stop and Rob." He sticks his pistol in the cashier's face and stammers, "OK —M-M-Mothersticker, t-t-t-this is a f- - - up!"

Unarmed countermeasures: Bill Rogers, the Director of the Institute of Advanced Weaponscraft, sums it up best for us. Rogers claims that for a bad guy to be successful he must have motivation and consciousness. Short circuit one or the other and you've just solved your immediate problem. So for starters your fighting skills need to give you the ability to quickly de-motivate your attacker and at least stun him long enough for you to escape safely (stun and run). Whatever you learn must also be capable of being applied very aggressively. Part of this is a time/endurance problem. You have at best 60 seconds to be all you can be. That's about as long as any of us can physically exert ourselves at full power. But the essential requirement for a combatives system is to put you in control of the situation. Dr. Paul Whitesell, a psychologist at the Ft. Wayne, Indiana Police Academy says it best in a research paper he prepared entitled, *The Psychology of Intimidation and Physical Conflict in the Police Profession.* "There are basically two types of attack: predatory and defensive. Predatory attack is very purposeful or directed. It is pronounced, offensive, dedicated, committed. Defensive aggression is frantic and wild."

So, for our hand-to-hand system, to meet these requirements it must be simple, effective, easy to learn, easy to retain. We must have confidence in our ability to apply it quickly, aggressively and offensively (in every sense of the word) under pressure. The techniques that we use must be designed to maximize our ability to quickly overwhelm (de-motivate and/or stun) our assailant. For my money, the embodiment of this concept is the "SEAL blitz," a technique developed for the U.S. Navy SEAL's by Paul Vunak. If you took Cooper's dictum that the best response to an attack on your person is an explosive violent counterattack and combined it with the Special Operations tactical principle of speed and violence of action, you now have a word picture of "the SEAL blitz." It is the most in-your-face right now, aggressive, "not today, you son-of-a-bitch!" technique I've ever seen. This is a purebred fighting animal. Every move is purposeful. Even in practice it looks like fighting, not dojo ballet. It was designed by a martial artist for non-martial artists. It was designed to give the little guy or gal a fighting chance against a larger and stronger opponent. Paul Vunak demonstrates it on his video, entitled "Street Safe," available from Threat Response Solutions, 2945 South Mooney Blvd., Visalia, California 93277 (1-800-899-81 53). Rick Faye, who heads the Minnesota Kali Group also demonstrates it on one of his videos. You can reach Rick at the Minnesota Kali Group, 328 East Hennepin Avenue, Suite 200, Minneapolis, Minnesota 55414 (612-331-6440).

   Oleoresin capsicum (O.C. or "pepper" spray): O.C. spray is one of the best tools available to us today. The latest study that I'm aware of on O.C. is the *Pepper Spray Evaluation Project* report dated 21 June 1995. It was a cooperative effort between the International Association of Chief's of Police and the Baltimore County (Maryland) Police Department under a grant funded by the National Institute of Justice. During this nine-month study the department had a total of 194 incidents in which O.C. was used. There were 174 incidents involving persons resisting arrest and 20 incidents involving dog attacks. A successful incident with a resisting subject was defined as one in which he or she was sufficiently incapacitated after a single spray to be placed under arrest. Using this guideline the spray was successful in 156 of the 174 incidents involving resisting subjects and in each of the incidents involving dogs. This produced an overall success ratio of 91%.

   Some of the other findings of this study which are of interest to us:

- Generally, if a suspect was sprayed with a one to three second burst from a distance of four to six feet he became submissive (if the spray is used at a closer distance it takes more time to work because the carrier concentration is heavier, the carrier is the type of liquid in your cannister)
- There is no indication that spraying more is better if the subject is properly sprayed the first time
- Proper use of the spray reduces the chance of injury to both the user and the attacker (because it minimizes contact while the subject is aggressive)
- Individuals who are heavily intoxicated, drugged and/or mentally ill may not be affected by O.C. spray and in fact may become more aggressive
- You need to have a backup option instantly available if the spray does not work
- O.C. spray is not a substitute for deadly force
- O.C. spray does not fit into a category or classification that would place it under the jurisdiction of any federal regulatory agency

O.C. spray is an excellent tool but because of the lack of product standards it is very brand specific. If you buy a brand that has no track record you may be disappointed in the results. The product used in this study was Bodyguard O.C. spray. The brand known as Capstun also appears to be quite effective. There are doubtless others. Just be sure you can obtain some usage data from an authoritative source. And make the effort to get trained in its use. O.C. spray has drawbacks just like anything else and you need to be aware of them. I suspect that for most of us this "karate in a can" will be the tool of choice in the less-than-lethal category to the exclusion of unarmed countermeasures and impact weapons so a good training course is a sound investment.

Impact weapons: Today this tool category includes the flashlight, the collapsible baton and the Kubotan. Of these I have found the flashlight to be the most useful (for me). I like the MagLite C (not D) cell style with a four-battery capacity. Before there was MagLite I carried a Safariland Kel-Light. The switch on the MagLite is better designed for carrying and is easier to manipulate with the various handgun flashlight techniques than the one on the Kel-Lite. These flashlights handle very much like the old style police straight baton and are super durable. Oh, and they also serve as a light source! I have lived in enough places with undependable electricity to be just a touch obsessive about having a good flashlight close at hand. There is an excellent text available on this versatile tool entitled *Defensive Tactics With Flashlights*, written by John Peters, the President of the Defensive Tactics Institute. You can obtain copies of his book by contacting John at P.O. Box 39, Millersville, Pennsylvania, 17551 (717-871-9860). It is a comprehensive examination of the subject and covers the legal aspects of defensive flashlight use, training techniques, flashlight handgun techniques, tactical flashlight use and so forth. The flashlight techniques are interchangeable with those of the collapsible baton.

Other than using it as a key flail to momentarily distract an assailant, I must admit to having little enthusiasm for the Kubotan. It reminds me of the old saying about the folly of poking short sticks at large dangerous animals. I am much more comfortable with the "big stick" approach.

Firearm/Vehicle: I'm not going to discuss firearms here since Dave will go into them in great detail in subsequent chapters. And we include the vehicle under lethal force options because that becomes a very real possibility when you start doing evasive maneuvers with something weighing several tons. I need to make this distinction because while we will not discuss using your car as a weapon, we are going to look at what you can do with it to extricate yourself from a carjacking.

This is a good place to reinforce the point that the sole purpose of motor skills training is to develop a conditioned response to a specific threat. You will have about a 3-5 second window in which to react to worst case situations. If you have to stop and think about what you are going to do you will simply run out of time.

Chapter 6

Survival Stress and the Conditioned Response

Survival stress is your body's mental and physical alarm reaction induced by a critical incident. The conditioned response is the learned reaction to a specific threat which presents itself during a critical incident. If your conditioned response is not practiced under simulated conditions, which induce survival stress you are probably not going to be really happy with your performance during a critical incident. This is where I side with those who believe that the 1,000 repetitions is a flawed concept. It is simply practice as opposed to skills installation. And a CRITICAL incident is one which threatens YOUR life. If it happens to someone else, it's just another incident. As in a parent telling the child, "This is going to hurt me as much as it hurts you." "Wanna trade places, Dad?"

Survival stress is induced in Condition Orange. When we become specifically alert to a threat. Consider as an example: There are ten more shopping days until Christmas. We leave the big discount store and walk to our car with both arms full of brightly colored packages. Catching movement out of the corner of our eye, we notice two men walking toward us. About three car lengths away they split up, one continuing in our direction, the other one moving along the line of cars working his way behind us...

About now, according to Bill Rogers, "Runaway anxiety may set in. Your heartbeat increases, your stomach knots up, your hands are cold and clammy, they may shake, you have the urge to urinate." If the situation allows us a Condition Orange we need to take full advantage of this time. This is our chance to come up with a plan while we can still think logically. So: We stop and set the packages on the car in front of us to free our hands and lighten our load. We turn so we can watch the progress of the two men. They stop. No words have been exchanged but something has passed between the three of you. The determination in your stance, the direct eye contact, some silent signal has told them that this one is not going to be easy. The evening is young. They can wait. There'll be others who are not so wary. The two men reverse their directions and walk away.

Or the situation may move so quickly that you are forced to react.

The intelligence officer was returning to his apartment after a memorable day on the golf course. He was tired but content. The day was a reminder of all that was good in the tiny African country to which he was assigned. What appeared to be a large bird sitting in the middle of the road snapped him out of his reverie. "Only in deepest darkest Africa," he chuckled to himself as he began braking to slow the vehicle. The deepening dusk and the absence of street lights prevented the officer from realizing that the "bird" was actually a man with a blanket draped over himself, until the car was almost on top of him. As the car continued to slow, the driver turned the steering wheel to avoid the man and drive around him. The man quickly side-stepped into the path of the oncoming car. Instantly the driver's training kicked in and he immediately turned his head to the left. Carjackers or kidnappers, the tactics are the same, his instructors told him during the personal security course he was required to attend prior to his overseas assignment. First they have to block the forward movement of your vehicle, then they'll come at you from the sides to get to the doors. But you're going to have another problem to deal with. One you'll face daily in most of the countries you'll be working in and that is how the locals drive normally. Which is, in a word, awful. So every time you drive you will see all sorts of weird and wonderful events that look like deliberate attempts to block your car. In reality, it's nothing personal, just how everyone there drives. To tell if you've got a problem, especially if you're involved in a fender bender, instantly check left, check right. If you see someone, or several someones running toward your car with guns, a reasonable and prudent man should assume that this is about to become one of those days his mother warned him about. By the time you see them you have already used up a large chunk of about a five-second window you have in which to react. Let's discuss your options and then we'll put you behind the wheel this afternoon and tonight and let you practice them. As if on cue, two men, or maybe it was three, stood up in the long grass which had concealed them, about three feet from the driver's door. One of them pointed a pistol at him. The officer stepped on the accelerator just as the gun fired.

In Condition Red survival stress is fully induced and a number of things happen simultaneously. Our heart rate leaps dramatically and as it goes over 145 beats per minute it dumps a protective chemical cocktail into our system. We lose our fine motor skills, our gross motor skills are enhanced, tunnel vision sets in, we lose depth perception and near vision, our mental processes speed up, we may experience auditory exclusion along with time and space distortion, and our subconscious takes over. We will react as we have been trained.

A number of researchers have developed a description of your mental processes at the onset of a critical incident. Siddle's is probably the best known.

1) Perceive the problem (.25 seconds)
2) Evaluate the problem (.25 seconds)
3) Select a response (.25 seconds)
4) Initiate the response (time depends on response selected)

However, I must admit that my favorite was designed by Dr. Roger M. Solomon, the department psychologist for the Washington State Patrol, and is explained in detail in the U.S. Department of Justice publication entitled *Police Psychology:*

Operational Assistance. According to Dr. Solomon this is how we really see the problem.

1) Welcome to Hell!
2) Oh S - - -!
3) Survive!
4) React!

It is important to note here that we are already at least three-fourths of a second behind the curve when the incident begins. This is why his actions always beat your reactions. You have, depending on the type of incident, at best 3-5 seconds in which to react. If you have no conditioned response, you'll get stuck at "React!" If you are not alert, you'll get stuck at "Oh S - - -!" Now we understand what is meant by the expression that "excitement won't kill us but surprise will."

This is also, I believe, the point at which our training can fail us or we can fail our training. Specifically, in the fight portion of the Fight, Flight or Freeze Syndrome we can experience major feelings of inadequacy. We can become fearful. We can lose our self-confidence. All of which leads to poor performance. We are not able to rise to the occasion. The fault generally lies in our mental preparation for a critical incident. Emptying your handgun at an adversary at close range without hitting him is an age-old example of this problem.

According to Rick Faye, who addresses this issue in his training programs, "most physically capable people can defend against a violent attack if:

1) They are aware of the attack in time.
2) They can attain the proper mental/physiological state.
3) They can remain focused and are not inhibited by pain or outside events.
4) They are trained in basic strategies and techniques."

Your training must be psychologically anchored. This ties the tactics and techniques to your body's natural fight or flight instincts.

Cooper tells us to turn fear into anger. Whitesell tells us the time to do this is when survival stress is induced in Condition Orange. "At the moment when the arousal (survival stress onset) is first noticed is the time to direct the spiral upward (turn anxiety into anger). The visceral effects of arousal can stir a motivation that no adversary would welcome . . . I believe that through training and preparation, we can prevent the psychological process from misinterpreting visceral awareness (survival stress onset) and starting a negative spiral (turning anxiety into fear). If one can get angry, or dedicate conscious thought to predatory aggressive demeanor while still in the aroused state of anxiety (you can enhance your survivability)."

This ability then, to learn how to access or "turn on" your fighting state WHILE IN TRAINING is the key to making survival stress work for you (not against you) in developing a dynamic conditioned response that will not fail you during a critical incident. This forces us to train from the neck up at the same time we are training from the neck down.

Chapter 7

Willingness

The officer worked for a small agency that bordered a high crime area of a large Midwestern city. He was an extremely active officer, always on the alert for people who did not "look right," cars that "did not belong" and for situations that did not fit into the immediate surroundings. He was highly effective and was praised for his high level of success. Unfortunately, along with his high success rate, came a certain arrogance. He had never yet met resistance, or at least that which he could not overcome, so he began to feel invincible.

One night, this officer was called to the rear of a shopping center on the report of a suspicious person prowling the area. The area was quite dark with only patches of light from dim bulbs above the rear doors of the stores. When the officer pulled in, he saw the suspect in question and called out to him to stop. The suspect walked off and did not look back. Instead of waiting for backup, the officer ran up behind the suspect, placed his hand on his shoulder, and spun him around. As the suspect turned, a gun appeared in his hand and he shot the officer in the abdomen. This officer later told me that he was so surprised by the action that he just fell down. Even though he was not incapacitated, he could not think to act.

The suspect ran away and was never caught. The officer recovered physically but not mentally. He later retired on a mental disability, unable to return to the street. What would have happened if the suspect had not run away? What would have happened if he had continued to attack? It is quite likely the officer would have perished instead of being retired. Being willing means to fight until the fight is over or there is nothing left to fight about.

Ed has made it quite clear to you that the mind is the body's most dangerous weapon. Without it everything else is for naught. Part of the definition we agreed on for the "Survivor's Attitude" is the willingness to do what you have to do. And we consider this attitude one of the three nonnegotiable components of personal safety for good reason. During my law enforcement career I have unfortunately seen too many cases, like the one above, in which the officer was both aware and trained. But at the moment of truth he was not willing. He could not bring himself to do what needed to be done. Consequently he did the exact opposite of our definition. He gave up. He became a victim.

Think about it. How many people out there do you know who may talk a good game or put up a good front, but you know in your heart they are not willing. I am concerned that I know more than I want to. I had a female cadet in a basic police academy class several years ago who was a good student. She listened well, did all the right things and had all the answers. She shot well on the range, performing quite well against paper targets. The problem began when she moved to the live fire house. The inside of the house was set up in a classic friend/foe building search with each target marked in such a way that the student had to decide who should be verbally confronted and who should be dealt with by using deadly force.

Some of the targets were paper, but others were life size, three dimensional Delta "human" targets. She opened the door tactically and moved around the door frame until she saw the target. At this point she froze. And I mean Froze! I had to call her name several times until I could get her to snap out of her haze. She holstered her Glock 19 9mm and turned toward me stating, "I'm sorry, but I don't think that I can shoot something that looks that much like a real human being." Her performance in the F.A.T.S. gunfight simulator was actually frightening. She could not bring herself to shoot at the film images of criminal suspects.

Dr. Alexis Artwohl, in her excellent book, *Deadly Force Encounters* (Paladin Press, 1997), discusses a study conducted by a law enforcement agency in which the police candidates were asked a question that required the use of deadly force. This question consisted of a scenario in which a fellow officer was being kicked to death and the candidate was on the other side of a high fence. The logical answer was to give a verbal warning and then deliver deadly force via the use of a firearm. Dr. Artwohl reported that two out of ten candidates WOULD NOT SHOOT, no matter what the circumstances!

So, what can we do to make sure we are ready, willing and able if our day comes. Dr. Artwohl makes the following recommendations:

- Stay up-to-date on tactics and techniques - Develop confidence backed by real skill. Know that your techniques will work.
- Practice mental imagery at least once a week.
- Learn what the physiological responses are to the fight or flight response and understand what will happen.
- Understand and accept that you may have to use deadly force.
- Strive to improve your observation and assessment skills
- Trust your instincts.
- Develop a powerful will to survive.
- Maintain a high level of physical fitness.
- Stay mentally positive.

Now, let's take a look at the real life example of Lance Thomas, someone who put these recommendations into practice. Although we have no way of knowing whether he read Dr. Artwohl's book, (if we assume that he did not) it is interesting that he reached some of the same conclusions on his own. Mr. Thomas was involved in four gunfights during which he killed five would-be robbers and wounded one. He was never prosecuted for any of these shootings. As you shall see, Mr. Thomas clearly understands the importance of willingness. The following is extracted from transcript number 133 of the ABC News show, "Turning Point," on *Guns and Self-Defense: When Can You Shoot*, aired 5 October, 1994.

Don Kladstrup: [Voice-over] For 14 years, Lance Thomas was a successful watch dealer in this West Los Angeles neighborhood, selling expensive, luxury and vintage watches. Five years ago, all that changed following a series of armed robberies in the area in which a number of shopkeepers were brutally murdered.

Lance Thomas: (Describing his first gunfight) " . . . I just decided not to be a victim in an instant. I'm not the fastest gun in the West. I'm not Wild Bill Hickok. I was scared to death. In fact, I thought I was . . . I could never make it."

Don Kladstrup: "In what way did it change your life?"

Lance Thomas: "That's how I came to looking at the whole picture of self-defense. What if . . . what if . . . what if. The scenarios were endless. And I found myself (planning), if it ever happened again, to (do whatever it took) to reduce the probability of losing my life."

Don Kladstrup: [Voice-over] Lance did that by practicing at the gun range, training at a gym several days a week and by working out gunfight tactics to every robbery scenario he could think of.

Don Kladstrup: (talking to Mr. Thomas about his second gunfight; Mr. Thomas' response is destined to become a classic) "How could you keep shooting, keep fighting back, with a bullet wound in the neck, three bullets in the shoulder?"

Lance Thomas: "They didn't kill me yet . . . and I hadn't run out of ammunition."

Don Kladstrup: [Voice-over] (talking about several other self-defense students he also interviewed) The question is, are they as mentally prepared to protect themselves as Lance Thomas was.

Lance Thomas: "Let's go all the way back mentally to ground zero. I'm faced with an armed intruder. Now, I have to make a mental decision to be a victim of his mercy or exercise the right of self-defense and fight back. And in fighting back, part of that is the willingness to die and to kill. Hard choice.

Richard Slotkin: (author of *Gunfighter Nation*) "Most people are not, in fact, willing to kill. Most people will hesitate before they pull the trigger. But the real edge in a gunfight is the one that's held by the more ruthless of the people that's in the gunfight, the one who is willing to kill without thinking twice about it, without wondering how he's going to feel after the fact . . . "

Don Kladstrup: [Voice-over] Certainly Lance Thomas believes that and has no remorse for the people he killed.

Lance Thomas: "Remorse and regret . . . if you look it up in the dictionary . . . is a connotation of error. I don't think I erred."

"WILL BEATS SKILL!"
>   - *Sam Faulkner, Ohio Peace Officer Training Academy*

"Most men, regardless of cause or need, aren't willing. They'll blink an eye or draw a breath before they pull the trigger and I won't."
- *John Wayne to Ron Howard in the 1976 film THE SHOOTIST*

Chapter 8

Legalities

Many years ago, I attended a pistol instructor course that was taught by one of the best-known firearms instructors in the world. While I found this training very worthwhile, one incident that occurred in the classroom portion has stayed with me. The instructor was giving an excellent lecture on how to deliver deadly force in a crisis situation. During the lecture, one student raised his hand and asked what should he expect from the criminal justice system after deadly force was used. The instructor stopped and looked at his student as if he had just landed on earth for the first time and said, "I'm here to teach you how to shoot, if you have legal problems hire a lawyer. That's what they're for."

I am afraid I must respectfully disagree. When dealing with the topic of self defense, I think it is absolutely essential to discuss what the person involved in such a situation can expect from the criminal justice system. This is especially true when it comes to a situation in which deadly force has been used. While surviving the confrontation is your ultimate goal, your personal liability cannot be ignored.

At this point, I feel it is very important to state that I am not a lawyer. I am a retired police officer. While I deal with the law, I do not interpret it. At the same time I do not want the reader to become so "liability phobic" that they will be afraid to respond when it is appropriate. I have come to believe that the American law enforcement community has reached this point. Needless to say, this "liability first" trend bothers me more than just a little bit.

Earlier, Ed spoke of the Use of Force Continuum. This is a tool that is used nationwide by law enforcement agencies to train their personnel in the proper use of force. As Ed explained, the continuum is basically a chart that says if the bad guy does this, the good guy should do that. Whatever option is used is based on a number of circumstances such as the good guy's level of training, available equipment, the number of bad guys, etc. The underlying message is that the action taken must be REASONABLE based on the circumstances at hand. If the good guy continues to use force after the attack has stopped, then he is facing some serious legal difficulties. In law enforcement circles, this principal is called the "reasonableness doctrine."

This doctrine has evolved out of numerous court cases, most all of which have involved the use of force by law enforcement officers. While it is true that law enforcement officials are agents of the government and will be judged to a higher standard than the average citizen, I feel it is safe to say that reasonableness will always be a factor anytime that violence is used in a self defense situation. It makes no difference whether the person involved is a police officer or legally armed citizen.

Your actions, whenever you defend yourself, will be judged on the basis of whether or not the action was reasonable based on the circumstances at hand. For example, the courts have ruled that deadly force should only be used when a person is facing a situation in which death or serious physical harm to himself or others could result if they do not act. Anything less than this is NOT considered reasonable.

Generally, for someone to place you in a position where you are in fear of death or serious bodily harm three things must be present:

1) Ability - Does the individual involved have the ability to cause serious physical harm or death? This usually means a weapon.

2) Opportunity - Is your assailant in a position to cause serious physical harm or death? This usually refers to distance.

3) Jeopardy - Has your assailant given you reason to believe that you are in fear of death or serious physical harm? This usually refers to his actions and/or what he says.

So what should you do if you are forced into a situation where deadly force is required? Well, expect to be treated like a suspect.

As a matter of fact, you ARE a suspect. You will be the center of a criminal investigation and you should think accordingly. You should do the following:

1) Remain at the scene and await the arrival of the police. Do not be in a threatening posture when they arrive.

2) Do not try and change the physical evidence at the scene. Trying to place a gun in the hands of an unarmed suspect will only get you into greater trouble. The level of forensic science in the 1990's will uncover such an unsophisticated attempt to modify evidence. The courts will be more understanding of an individual who killed in error out of fear or panic than a person who tries to tamper with evidence.

3) Do not say anything. The police may say that they need your statement to proceed with their investigation, but this is not true. Homicides are investigated every day with the most important witness being deceased. It is best to make a short statement such as, "He tried to kill me, and I had to shoot." Then ask for a lawyer. There is nothing wrong with heading the police in the right direction, but don't say anything you are likely to regret. You have the right to remain silent. Use it!

4) Ask for a lawyer. This is your right. Find a lawyer who understands the dynamics of use of force cases. Find out who the police in your area use and have his or her card on hand. Even if you are totally in the right, you will need to talk to a lawyer if for nothing else, to get your facts straight after the incident. You must remember that you will be coming down after an extreme adrenaline rush and will not be thinking clearly. Talking with a lawyer will help you get your story straight, as well as compose yourself, before you give the police an official statement.

Chapter 9

Medical Self-help

Like the chapters on driving, most of what you read in this chapter was written by a subject matter expert. (In other words, not me!) In this instance an Emergency Medical Technician friend of mine with about fifteen years of experience in the field. His hard-earned expertise was gained on assignments ranging from a military field medic in third world low intensity conflicts to medical officer for dignitary protection details. His current job allows him to practice, teach and study emergency medical techniques. I hope you'll find his advice as helpful as I do.

I first learned of the self-help concept during my military service some 30 years ago. A grizzled old Special Forces Major who had paid his dues in WWII, Korea and Vietnam told us that we had to be prepared to take care of ourselves if we were ever cut off from our unit. He claimed that one of his biggest concerns was having to treat a gaping wound until he could either get picked up or make it back to a safe area. At which time he said, "This is why I always carry these," and he pulled a string of safety pins, the big black military issue kind, from a pocket. "This will suture me up just fine." I am here to tell you he really got my attention because there was no way Mrs. Lovette's little boy was gonna' sew himself up with safety pins! I couldn't rest until I found (for me) a better solution (duct tape). Today I am convinced that self-help is one of the most essential and at the same time most overlooked skills, not only for those interested in personal protection, but also for those whose profession requires them to go in harm's way. The implication here seems to be that if you are involved in an armed encounter only the other guy will get hurt. The existence of concealable soft body armor is an admission that we are not immune to injury but that is usually about as far as the preparation goes. Consequently, finding information that deals with treating yourself in the event of serious injury is rare. Surprisingly, finding qualified medical personnel with an interest in self-aid is not easy. Not recognizing this as an important issue and learning what to do about it has lead to panic, shock and death in emergency situations. How else do you explain the death of an otherwise healthy individual who dies at the scene from a non-fatal bullet wound to an extremity?

So, what we're talking about here is the ability to provide immediate, temporary care to yourself for serious injuries you may sustain as the result of your involvement in a critical incident. Obviously, you use the same techniques on yourself that you would use on someone else. Given the response times in most jurisdictions we would ideally like for you to be able to stabilize yourself for about 15 minutes. The reality may be considerably longer.

As the young officer walked up to the vehicle he had just pulled over there was no indication that this was anything other than a routine stop for a traffic violation. Although new to the department, he had done this many times, both with his field training officer and, more recently, on his own. His most graphic memory of the event is that the driver's side of the car appeared to light up. He went down instantly and it was only as the vehicle sped away that he realized he'd been shot. He had seen combat duty during his military service and he knew that whatever else he did, he couldn't allow himself to lose consciousness. He dragged himself back to his patrol car and found, after opening the door, he could not pull himself into the vehicle. Fortunately, he had left the microphone on the seat and he was able to reach it. Clamping his leg with one hand to stop the flow of blood from a punctured femoral artery, he talked slowly and distinctly into the microphone, giving the dispatcher his location and the extent of his injuries, and then repeating over and over to her, "Keep talking to me . . . don't let me pass out." The last thing he remembers saying to her is, "I can hear sirens . . . The medics said he was barely

conscious when they got there and that he passed out as
soon as they began to work on him. Within three months he
was back on the street.

As we have stated elsewhere, this is not intended to be a "how to" manual. If you wish to learn or improve your first aid skills you need to take advantage of the resources available in your area. What we are going to talk about is intended to give you a procedure which can serve as a guide during the period of time you may have to tend to yourself. It is based on the standard ABC's of emergency care: Airway - check the airway, Breathing - check the breathing, Circulation - stop the bleeding. Since most everyone has probably been exposed to the ABC's in some previous first-aid training, my EMT friend elected to stay with this format and expand it. We're going to call this our Primary Survey. In keeping with the time-honored KISS principle our Secondary Survey will be to keep repeating the Primary Survey until help arrives. One of the major benefits of the Primary Survey - Secondary Survey process is that it helps focus your thinking on a positive outcome. Willingness (Chapter 7) goes both ways. I WILL SURVIVE!

Shots have been fired. One of your assailants is down and the other has fled. You need to reload. You need to call the cops. And then you realize the front of your shirt is soaked with blood. You know you cannot, must not panic . . . First, get into a position that will allow you to be as comfortable as possible and also permits you to breathe easily. Then:

A.   Assess the situation: (if you're working on someone else "A" stands for airway. When you're working on yourself if you can think rationally your airway is functioning adequately). Make appropriate use of your time. Do I treat myself first and then get on the phone? Where is the phone? Do I even have a cotton-pickin' phone!? Am I sure that my assailant is no longer a threat?

B.   Breathing: Control your breathing. Slowing down the rate of respiration will help alleviate the "adrenaline rush" that has occurred and will help to slow down the heart rate. Consciously deep breathing in and out through the nose is a good way to accomplish this. Trouble breathing may indicate lung damage.

C. Circulation: Are you bleeding? If so, where and how bad? Control the bleeding immediately with any means that you have available. Apply direct pressure with your hand, a sanitary napkin, clothing or other available material. Do not worry about sterility at this time. The bleeding must be controlled to preclude further deterioration and shock which will render you incapable of providing further treatment to yourself.

D. Disability (mental and physical): What happened? Where are you? How bad are you hurt? Can you move? Are you still in danger? Remember that you are probably experiencing the physiological effects that result from any critical incident. These include rapid heart rate, increased rate of respiration and heightened awareness. Be aware that these are natural, normal, predictable reactions and do not let them cloud good judgment. Simply said, you're trying to work through the effects of mental and physical tunnel vision.

E. Examine: Examine yourself to find other wounds that you may have missed. (If you have a hole in front, check to see if you have a hole in back.)

F. Five senses: Can you see? Can you hear? Can you feel? Can you smell? Can you taste?

REPEAT UNTIL HELP ARRIVES: A-B-C-D-E-F:
ASSESS – **B**REATHING - **C**IRCULATION - **D**ISABILITY - **E**XAMINE - **F**IVE SENSES

Under these circumstances a pre-positioned first aid kit with which you are thoroughly familiar can prove invaluable. Such kits should be in keeping with our philosophy of what a lone individual can do on the street, in a vehicle or in the home. Since medical kits tend to contain items based on personal experience, medical history, training and so on, we're going to spend more time on the commonalities that these kits should have rather than the differences.

For starters, all kits must be readily accessible. If you can't get to it, the kit is useless. Everyone who potentially might use the kit must know how to use all the equipment in it. Keep in mind that the elements, heat, wind, rain, sand etc., can degrade, damage or render your kit inoperable. Check your kit contents regularly. Keep the kit simple. In the type of scenario we are dealing with, the simpler the better.

Four common items are essential to each of these kits. You must have some form of communication, a light source, a pocket tool or knife and the medical supplies themselves. Communication in a self-aid situation is quite literally our lifeline. We may shout, throw a rock through someone's window or dial a cell phone, but we need to get help. A light source may be a pack of matches or a flashlight. It can help you see and can help others see you. Another important item that each kit should have is a pocket tool or knife. The choice is yours. Between a Leatherman style "tool plier" and a Swiss Army knife you can deal with most any self-aid situation. And finally, no matter what else you have in the way of medical supplies, you must have a blood stopper (this may be anything from your tee shirt to a commercial sterilized wound dressing) and of course, duct tape. From sucking chest wounds to splinting fractures, if you only have the use of one hand and your teeth, etc., keep a roll handy.

Below you will find several sources for these kits. Whether you purchase them already packaged or make your own, our only suggestion is that if you need training, do that first. It will help you make informed decisions about what to put in your kits and very likely will introduce you to people who can serve as your resource for future guidance or who will put you in touch with someone who can.

Probably the least expensive sources that provide good quality are K-Mart and Wal-Mart. From Campmor (P.O. Box 700-P, Saddle River, New Jersey 07458-0700, 1-800-226-7667) you can obtain Adventure Medical Kits developed by Dr. Eric A. Weiss. They come in sizes like Trail, Day Tripper, Weekender and so on. Campmor also carries Dr. Weiss' book on field and emergency medicine which is extremely well written. A new source of excellent self-help first aid kits is ProMed Kits (800-776-5310). These kits were developed by Dave Cruz, a former U.S. Air Force Para-Rescue Jumper (PJ), and are perfect for this type of life saving situation. Also specific types of medical supplies can be purchased from DYNAMED medical products (1-800-854-2706).

Bottom line? With good training and the will to survive you don't need fancy equipment. With a cell phone, a mini-Maglite, a Swiss Army knife, some sanitary napkins and some duct tape you'll do just fine. And you won't have to worry about those @#%*II safety pins!

Chapter 10

You and Your Vehicle

I had a lot of help in assembling this chapter and the one that follows it. The folks who did most of the work on them are experts in this particular field (offensive/defensive driving, sometimes also referred to as evasive driving) and have an impressive record of "saves" in some pretty hostile environments. One of their observations that I found particularly noteworthy was that it is a shame that good, affordable driving schools are not as common as good shooting schools. This seems to be a major deficiency in commercially available personal security training for the private citizen. Too bad, because driving skills are used daily and the chances of you using your car to avoid-evade-counter have a higher probability than your use of firearms.

The woman was stopped at a traffic light with a lane of traffic on either side of her. It was about 6:30 in the morning and she was on her way to work. She glanced casually at the rearview mirror and was about to look away when she noted a man walking up to the line of vehicles behind her. As she watched, he attempted to open the driver's door of one of the cars. She checked quickly to make sure her own doors were locked and the windows were rolled up. She again checked the mirror and saw that the man had now moved up the line of cars and was two vehicles in back of her still trying find an unlocked driver's door. Blocked on all four sides by rush hour traffic she started frantically blowing the car's horn and flashing her headlights just as the man approached her door. He looked at her as if trying to decide what to do next, then slowly turned and began running into the housing area adjacent to the roadway. Her actions had alerted a passing patrol

car (who says you can't find a cop when you need one) and
he was able to apprehend the individual.

The average American driver spends approximately 38 minutes behind the wheel of his car every day. Yet, according to Tony Scotti, the former President of Scotti's School of Defensive Driving, most drivers consider their car pretty much as they do their living room sofa. They are capable of using about 50% of the vehicle's performance. Think about that. Most cars you see in traffic are right on the rear bumper of the car in front of them. The driver is staring straight ahead, day dreaming. He may be drinking a cup of coffee (or a giant soft drink in a cup large enough to obscure their vision even when they are not drinking from it), reading a newspaper, balancing a checkbook, talking on the car phone, putting on their makeup, performing mouth-to-mouth resuscitation on their seatmate (well that's what it looked like to me), or my personal favorite, flossing. Yes, with both hands. While steering the car with her knees.

As with shooting, you can't master the skills you need to enhance your security while driving simply by reading a book. But it ain't a bad place to start. The good news is, unlike shooting, once you learn the necessary driving skills you can practice most of them daily. A good driving program then must address: 1) the driver, 2) the vehicle, and (how they relate to and interact with), 3) the environment. We're going to focus mostly on the driver and the vehicle since there's not much you can do about the environment (weather, road surface, traffic conditions).

Be alert, and aware, watch everything going on in your 360°/21' bubble and use massive doses of common sense. The basics still apply. We're just adding the car. The car now becomes a tool which permits you to avoid-evade-counter, assuming you do your part. Remember, it is not the limitations of the vehicle that determine the boundaries of performance, it is the limitations of the driver. The really good news is that if you have been driving (legally) since you were sixteen or so you probably already can perform the skills that will get you out of most situations. Our studies have identified these skills as going forward (lane clear, lane blocked), going backward, making a U-turn, doing a curb jump or a tire drop. Forget the exotic stuff. Leave it to the movies. We'll discuss this in detail later.

For now, before we even get in the car we need to remind ourselves to watch who is around the vehicle as we walk up to it. Check under it before we get close to the vehicle and look into it before we get in. Where possible the car should be parked so we can get in and drive off without having to back up. And as part of this sequence, as soon as we get into the car before we put the key into the ignition we should make sure the doors are locked and the windows are up.

Now we can take a look at the car. First the outside. The two most critical things here are good mirrors and good tires. Mirrors should be positioned to allow the greatest range of vision. A small stick-on convex mirror on the driver's side mirror and one on the passenger's mirror, in combination with the interior rear view mirror will give you close to a 360-degree field of view. The stick-on mirrors cost about two dollars at many convenience stores.

Next tires. My friends wrote a mountain of stuff on tires. Since this is not a book about tires, I've condensed their info considerably but not their message. TIRES ARE IMPORTANT! Consider that a car is really designed to do three things: go, stop and turn. Ultimately, the thing that makes a car go, stop and turn is the friction between that part of the tire in contact with the road (the contact patch) and the road surface. To over simplify slightly, the quickest that you can accelerate is to that point just short of your tires spinning. As much as some of us thought that spinning our tires when the light changes thoroughly impressed all who could see, hear and smell the burning rubber, an acceleration skid serves no purpose. The most efficiently you can brake is the point just short of your tire skidding. This is the advantage of anti-lock braking systems (ABS). The fastest that you can negotiate a given corner is that speed just short of either the front or rear tires sliding sideways. Thinking of it this way, we can say that high performance driving is basically traction management.

Second part of the tire message. It is NOT necessary to purchase high performance tires for your car if it does not already have them. Even if you are required to evade, it should be for a short distance – from where you first start the evasion to the nearest safe place. Our big concern is TRACTION MANAGEMENT. In order to maximize traction, we must maximize the amount of rubber in contact with the road surface. Some people assume that it is the grooves in the tread that provide traction. In fact, on a dry surface, the tread reduces traction. That is why race cars use smooth tires ("slicks") on a dry race track. The only function of the grooves on pavement is to channel the water out from under the rubber that must stay in contact with the road.

Third important part of the message. Proper tire inflation is critical if you are ever going to demand "performance" from your vehicle. Therefore, the first, AND PROBABLY ONLY NECESSARY speed improvement that we should make on any car that may possibly be used in high performance or emergency situations is to properly inflate the tires. In order to maximize traction (and handling), we recommend that non-speed rated tires be inflated to four or five pounds over the maximum pressure ratings embossed on the sidewalls of the tires on your car. If the tires are speed rated, this additional pressure has already been taken into account.

Moving from the outside of the vehicle to under the hood, we need to take care of oil, water, brake fluid, transmission fluid, window washing fluid, and so forth during routine maintenance checks. Ideally we should always have at least a half tank of gas.

Inside the car we need to acquaint ourselves with door and window locks and how they function and likewise the seatbelt. Panel lighting should be the least amount you need to easily read the gauges. Many of us don't seat ourselves properly in the car. We tend to recline our seat backs because it is intuitively more comfortable to do so. The problem is that it desensitizes our bodies to various forces which we should use to communicate with the car. If we sit erect, we are more sensitive to vibrations, and acceleration, deceleration and cornering forces. Sitting erect also makes us tired less quickly than reclining does.

You should be seated close enough to the wheel to allow you to place your wrist on top of the wheel, have a slight bend at the elbow, and keep your shoulders against the seat back. There is a great deal of debate about whether the hands should be at 10:00 and 2:00 or 3:00 and 9:00. We prefer the 9 and 3 because our experience has shown that the 10 and 2 driver tends to allow his hands to progressively come closer and closer together on the steering wheel. (As an experiment, place your hands side-by-side and see how smoothly you can steer. Then place your hands as far apart as possible on the wheel and see how smoothly you can steer). The driver who normally drives with his hands at 9 and 3 is more likely to keep his hands far apart as he corners.

Just so we don't get bogged down in detail here, hand placement is important as it relates to your ability to drive smoothly. Smoothness is everything. In order to maintain traction you MUST drive smoothly. In fact, this may be the single most important factor in being able to drive fast. Smooth drivers can drive fast. Jerky drivers cannot. Smooth driving means smooth inputs applied to all of the cars controls.

You should also be able to place your foot at the full range of the pedals without having to stretch. Rather than placing your right foot on the accelerator when you get into the car, you should first place your foot comfortably on the brake pedal, with the heel resting on the floorboard directly beneath the toes. The toes - not the ball or arch of the foot should be on the brake pedal. To accelerate, simply pivot your foot on the heel and press against the gas pedal without lifting or moving your heel. When it becomes necessary to brake, simply rotate your foot and without raising your heel off the floorboard, place your toes on the brake pedal and apply the appropriate pressure. You will find that you can do this much more quickly than raising your foot from the gas pedal, moving it over to the brake pedal, and lowering it onto the brake. Experience has shown that it will take about two weeks of practice for drivers who are accustomed to lifting their foot to get into the habit of simply rotating it.

Now, we can go for a spin.

Chapter 11

Behind the Wheel

One of the toughest things to deal with in our daily driving is the boredom of routine. There is a tendency to let the car drive itself while we solve problems at the office or daydream (remember Scotti's sofa?). We see the results of this daily along the roadside as drivers exchange insurance company phone numbers while waiting for the police and/or the tow truck. An aid for this problem, which helps you stay alert and is also a handy way to learn a new area quickly is called "commentary driving" (talking aloud to ourselves about what we see as we drive). Commentary driving helps us to respond to what we see both visually (passively) and orally (actively). Because we now see, say and hear ourselves say what we are seeing, we have employed more than one of our senses. This technique can be extremely helpful in forcing us to remember what we see. It is amazing how much more quickly you can become familiar with a new area using commentary driving. As we get comfortable with it, you will also notice potential problems sooner.

This is useful because eventually we need to reach the point where all of the actions that we take inside of the car are automatic (Just like our gun handling skills). Only then can we devote our entire attention to what is happening outside of the car. In the previous chapter we said that smooth driving means smooth inputs applied to all the car's controls.

So let's start with steering. There is a very simple secret to steering smoothly. An experiment will dramatically illustrate the value of this technique. Find a deserted section of road. With someone in the passenger's seat to warn you of oncoming traffic, pedestrians, etc., stare at the road just beyond your hood and concentrate on staying in the center of your lane as you drive. After a minute or so, take note of how much input you are putting into the steering wheel. You will find that you are driving like most new drivers - constantly overcorrecting. Now look as far as you can to your front, even to where the road disappears on the horizon or as far around the next curve as you can see. After a minute or two of driving this way, take note of how little steering input is required. Hopefully, you will find that your steering input is much smoother when you are looking far to the front. The added advantages of looking far to the front when you are attempting to spot potential threats should be obvious. You will also notice that you will see everything that takes place between you and the farthest distance you can see. If you are looking only as far as the taillights of the car in front of you, you will not see anything that takes place beyond that car. If you are looking at the point where the road disappears, you will certainly see the taillights of all the cars on the road ahead of you. (Note: Once you are ready to try this in traffic, start with our 21'/360° rule in slow rush hour traffic. Watch the car in front of the vehicle immediately in front of yours to increase your reaction time. As you increase your speed, keep this simple formula in mind. Take half of whatever speed is indicated on your speedometer and add it to your actual speed. For example, half of 60 MPH is 30 MPH. 60 MPH + 30 MPH = 90 FEET PER SECOND. MPH is kinda' hard to grasp but FPS is pretty clear. That's how fast you're going. When you figure how many car lengths this is, and reaction time, plus the skid factor, well you get the message. "DON'T TAILGATE" has to be one of the most understated rules of the road.)

The intelligence officer was en route to pick up some equipment. He was concerned not only with the usually lousy traffic conditions but also with the sluggishness of the diesel truck he was driving. He had to plan every turn and lane change he made because the truck had zero acceleration. To add to the good news he was in a country that drove in the left lane. For all these reasons (plus his training as he was to tell us later) he was looking as far down the road as he could when he began the left turn into a side street. He instantly keyed on the three young men standing on the left side of the roadway. It suddenly dawned on him as he began to slow the truck to make the turn that they were just as intently watching HIM. He was still braking and beginning to make the turn when Lady Luck intervened. He saw one of the men raise his hand and point a handgun at him. (If the shooter had waited about two seconds more, the outcome would have been totally different.) The officer slammed on the brakes, threw the truck in reverse, and stood on the accelerator. The surprised gunman did not fire until the truck started backing away from him and a single round struck the windshield. The driver backed up until he was far enough away to turn the truck around. Fortunately for him, because as soon as he yanked the steering wheel to begin the turn the truck, it stalled. (Not uncommon in reverse 180's or bootlegger spins done at speed. Not to mention broken down third world diesels.) Lady Luck still smiled. He got the truck started again and left the scene at a very low rate of speed.

Now let's look at smooth braking. In an emergency driving situation we may need to slow down or stop quickly. The problem with standing on the brake is that we may lock them up. When the brakes lock we lose steering control, much like skidding on an icy roadway. Hence, anti-lock braking systems or ABS, which prevent brake lockup.

But what do we do if our car has conventional brakes? Many of us were taught to pump the brakes in an emergency stop. Using this method, we alternately lock and unlock the brakes. While the brakes are locked, we lose steering control. We sacrifice traction management. We can only steer the car when we release brake pressure.

A much better technique for conventional brakes is to apply just enough pressure to the brake to be at the point, or threshold, just before lockup. In fact, the technique is called "threshold" braking. The wheels never lock up so complete control is retained throughout the process of slowing or stopping. With practice threshold braking will allow you to stop in about half the distance required for pumping the brakes with no loss in steering control.

The point of all that we have discussed up to now should be obvious. If you can steer, brake, accelerate and backup smoothly you can extract yourself from the majority of street crimes you will encounter while driving. Said another way, you already have the necessary skills. We just want to help you do them more smoothly because smooth is fast. The most often employed evasive driving maneuvers are going forward, going backwards and U-turns. As part of going forward you may have to steer around an obstacle blocking the lane in front of you. This might require you to drive over a curb (curb jump) or to drive off the roadway (tire drop).

But what about the fun stuff that 007 uses? Bootlegger spins and "J" turns, sometimes referred to as forward and reverse 180's. For starters, finding situations in which people trained in these techniques actually used them are rare. The reasons are pretty much the same ones that explain why complex motor skills degrade or fail under stress. Too many steps, timing, independent hand and foot movements which must be coordinated and no room for error. Throw in the variables of traffic, road conditions, stick shift, right-hand drive, familiarity with the vehicle you are driving and frequency of practice and you'll see why we feel these techniques are best left to the movies. There are a number of other more practical skills, such as ramming another vehicle, which are beyond the scope of this book.

So what are some of the things we can do. It is important that we get our priorities straight. Remember that the car is a weapon. Surprising how many folks feel that they are armed only when carrying a handgun. And if you have a problem or see a problem developing, do something. Don't just sit there. A moving vehicle is tough to stop. Vehicles are like tanks. They can sustain substantial body damage, flat tires and blown radiators and still keep moving while soaking up bullets, especially pistol bullets, like a sponge. Ask any cop who has tried to stop a fleeing vehicle with his duty sidearm.

Always have an exit. Just like the pilot who is always looking for a place to put his plane down in an emergency. If you're stopped far enough behind the car in front of you so that you can see its rear tires, you have room to maneuver. ("What if . . . Where can I drive through or around?") If you look at your exit and drive towards it, you'll do just fine.

Interestingly, we have found if you look at the obstacle and try to steer around it you'll invariably oversteer or hit the object. If you can't move or if the problem is in the car with you, the gun now becomes an option.

Like the cowboy's horse, your vehicle can be a faithful companion in good times and bad.

Chapter 12

Living With Terrorism

These next two chapters were taken from my column in *Combat Handguns* following the 9-11 attack and have been reworked for this book.

The awareness skills required to spot terrorist surveillance, or other activities that they might conduct during their planning and preparation stages of an operation, are an extension of what you need to do to deal with a criminal threat. The big difference between the danger signs signaling an imminent criminal assault and the precursors for a terrorist attack in the planning and preparation stages, is time. A criminal assault is usually measured in seconds from start to finish while a terrorist attack may be years in the planning. The shortest planning time that we can document for a particular group that specialized in kidnap and assassination was about 30 days. Al-Qaeda may take from 18 months to 5 years.

While I certainly got an education in terrorism during my Agency career, I do not consider myself an expert on the subject. I am much more comfortable with an observation I saw on a TV news show that discussed the impact of 9-11 on America. The report claimed that all Americans were now veterans of terrorism. I, like you, am a terrorism veteran. The only difference is the number of campaigns we have under our belts. So what I am about to share with you, you may already know or have already read. Terrorism has been with us long enough for some very bright people to have said nearly everything worth saying about it. I'm just borrowing their words.

I first became interested in terrorism in the late 1970's. The experts predicted that low intensity conflict, which included terrorism, was the type of warfare we would be confronting and it would be with us for a long time to come. I read everything I could find on the subject, but I must confess that trying to understand the dynamics of terrorism, especially with its alphabet soup of groups and their philosophies and intentions, frankly was more than I could handle. What helped me was to simplify the subject, as I do with most things that appear complicated, by breaking it up into easily digested bite-sized pieces.

Remember the 1970's when airline hijackings were all the rage? Remember Entebbe? Remember Mogadishu? Well it didn't seem to me those incidents were having much effect on anything. What was the point? I was sent to a terrorism seminar sponsored by the Illinois State Police. During one of the classes I asked the instructor how we could tell if/when terrorism was succeeding. His response was, "When it begins to affect the quality of your life." Until the 11th of September 2001, terrorism in the U.S. had not significantly affected the quality of our lives. We can no longer make that claim. We have lost our innocence. We have joined the long list of other nations who have been living with terrorism for years. Hopefully, one of the positive results of this attack will be to band us together to defeat a common foe.

There is a great deal of wisdom in the phrase that you don't hear very often: "Terrorists are not ten feet tall." Because we don't understand them and why they commit such atrocious acts of violence, there is a tendency to make more of them than they are. They are often portrayed as some sort of cult-like slippery evil spirits. This was especially true during the 1970's when the threat of terrorism began to rear its ugly head. There were many groups that tended to do their own thing. They each carried their own banner, so to speak. We didn't know much about them, but the lesson we most certainly learned from their bloody deeds in those early days, was the power of terrorism. You could not watch a terrorist act on the nightly news and not in some way be touched by it. The experts would explain this to us with phrases such as, "Terrorism is the weapon of the weak against the strong." "Terrorism is theater." "The purpose of terrorism is to terrorize." But it still did not have much impact on us. It was something that happened "over there" and rarely targeted Americans. That was then, this is now.

I think most historians can agree that this all changed on 18 April 1983, with the first U.S Embassy bombing in Beirut, Lebanon. Terrorism, as we know it today, began on that date, almost 20 years before 9-11. I know it was my wakeup call. I had just left Beirut about 10 days earlier. I knew and worked with almost everyone the Agency lost in that bombing. Islamic extremists had declared war on America. To keep this brief we must skip over an awful lot of awful history to get to the next significant date, 26 February 1993. That is the date that Islamic extremists conducted the first attack on the World Trade Center. That date is significant because, although Al-Qaeda was not organized in its current form until 1995, it is generally agreed that Osama Bin Laden and the ideology that would give rise to Al-Qaeda are credited with inspiring this attack against the U.S. If we add to his list of attacks against us the U.S. Air Force barracks at Khobar Towers (Saudi Arabia), the attack on the USS Cole, the two U.S. Embassy bombings in Africa, plus a couple of other operations we disrupted, we are now almost to 9-11.

It is important for us to understand that during this time Bin Laden was training thousands of future terrorists in Afghanistan. I've seen figures ranging from 10,000 to 50,000 that went through these camps. They were from many countries to which they returned after the training. The point here is that Bin Laden made his terrorist effort truly global. There exists today a better trained, better organized, more effective terror network than any we have had to deal with before because of his efforts. Both the FBI and the CIA agree that the most serious threat facing our country today is posed by Al-Qaeda, Bin Laden's organization.

Which brings us to 9-11. For all of us in this country it would be a truly horrific event. It would be yet another attack on us by Islamic extremists. It would be the biggest attack ever in the U.S. It would be Bin Laden's most spectacular attack ever. As a nation and as a people, the 9-11 attack would change us forever. It would leave us all trying to understand, and explain to our children, a group of people who hate us more than they love life. (For a better understanding of who these people are and why they believe what they believe you need to read Tom Friedman's *Longitudes and*

Attitudes). And it showed us for the first time, what we are truly up against. We have had commissions, news specials, political analysts and so on repeatedly tell us that we should have seen this coming. We missed it. To put this in context, we need to understand that while we did indeed miss it, so did the Brits, the Israelis, the Germans, et al. Al-Qaeda operations are characterized by meticulous planning and impressive operational security. But the most significant result of the 9-11 attack was that the U.S. finally declared war on terrorism, almost 20 years after they first attacked us.

Probably the toughest thing that many of us are going to have to do in this war is to come to grips with a people and a philosophy that are at the opposite end of the spectrum from how we look at life. We are going to have to understand that we are now in a war, which we must win, against a foe that has flown, not one but two, airliners into a building full of innocent human beings. We are going to have to "put on our game face" and do what is necessary against a people and a philosophy that kidnaps innocent non-combatants and beheads them. We are going to have to "get our head right" against a people and a philosophy that sees nothing wrong with conducting a full-scale military operation against a school and randomly murdering several hundred children, the future of that (or any) country.

But we must do it and we can do it. In the opening moments of this war, even as the attacks against this great democracy were taking place, a tiny group of Americans became the first heroes of the war. They would not be bullied. They demonstrated that they too were willing to give their lives without hesitation for a cause they believed in. They showed armed murderers what happens when you poke short sticks at a large dangerous animal. Raw courage, true grit and bare knuckles. How fittingly American… We must ensure that the spirit of United Airlines flight 93 sustains us in the coming fight. As someone said of those heroic American patriots, "They will always serve as a reminder to us that courage is what fear becomes after you've said your prayers."

So, we the people are going to make the difference in this war. We are going to have to be tough-minded. The best example I have of this is a tactic that I am told is standard practice by the British SAS. When they clear a building everyone who races past a downed terrorist is required to shoot them again. This ensures that the bad guy will not be able to get away or shoot one of the team in the back. This is a small example of what we are going to have to do on a very large scale. We need to support those who will take the fight to the enemy—starting with each other and our community, in conjunction with the intelligence community, the law enforcement community and our Armed Forces.

We cannot shrink from this challenge. We are going to have to be resolute. My favorite explanation of this comes from the movie "The Untouchables." Kevin Costner is trying to recruit Sean Connery to assist him with his attempt to bring down Al Capone. Connery tells Costner, "If you are going to open the ball on these people you must be prepared to go all the way. They won't stop the fight until one of you is dead. If he pulls a knife, you pull a gun. If he sends one of yours to a hospital you send one of his to the morgue." This is another way of saying that we are facing an enemy you cannot negotiate with.

Someone sent me a copy of a speech prepared by Dr. Tony Kern, a retired Air Force Lt. Col. who was the former Director of Military History at the Air Force Academy. I'd like to share a portion of this with you:

> *The Prussian General, Carl von Clausewitz, says that there is a remarkable trinity of war that is composed of, 1) the will of the people; 2) the political leadership of the government; and 3) the chance and probability that plays out on the field of battle, in that order. Every American citizen was in the crosshairs of that Tuesday's attack, not just those who were unfortunate enough to be in the World Trade Center or the Pentagon. The will of the American people will decide this war. If we are to win, it will be because we have what it takes to persevere through a few more hits, learn from our mistakes, improvise and adapt. If we can do that*

we will eventually prevail. Everyone I have talked to in the last few days has shared a common frustration, saying in one form or another, "I just want to do something!" You are already doing it. Just keep faith in America, and continue to support your President and the military, and the outcome is certain. If we fail to do so, the outcome is equally certain. God Bless America.

Chapter 13

What Can I Do?

The short answer to the question posed by this chapter title is, **Be alert. If you see suspicious activity report it to the authorities.** A recent newspaper article entitled, *America's New War*, claimed that the U.S. will wage this war on five fronts. These are Diplomatic, Financial, Intelligence, Military and Law Enforcement. I think they left out a sixth front that's of equal importance, and that is the Home Front, the good ol' U.S. of A. I'm not speaking here of the new Department of Homeland Security, I'm talking about our role, the role of the American citizen, in a war in which one man, woman or child can make a difference. While this may be America's new war, a number of other countries have lived with the terrorist threat for a good many years. History shows us that there are three of the above fronts that are everywhere engaged in this war 24/7/365. They are Intelligence, Law Enforcement and the citizens who comprise the Home Front.

Consider the following example taken from a book which I have found to be one of my most useful resources on the role of the individual who must live in an active terrorist environment. It is entitled *Diplomats and Terrorists II, Overseas Security: Our People Are the Key* by Harold G. Bean. It underscores the extent to which individual and collective awareness can pay off. *The central bus station in Tel Aviv is awash with humanity: old women with shopping bags, young men in short jackets, Israeli soldiers with automatic weapons, Palestinian laborers, rabbis. They have one habit in common, however: When they board a bus, they glance under the seat and in the overhead rack, checking for suspicious packages. Officials of the Israeli Defense Forces say that more than 80% of bombs in public places are dismantled because of the awareness of the public that there is such a thing as a suspicious object.*

In *Defensive Living*, Dave and I discuss the importance of awareness with respect to your personal security. Our main concern is with street crime. The terrorist threat requires us to use these same skills while looking for different indicators. Some may be as obvious as the guy in the seat across the aisle on your flight striking a match and holding it to his shoe. (Can you believe that?) Or the individual who goes to a flight school and tells them he wants to learn to take-off and fly a plane but he doesn't need the lessons on how to land it. (Hello!?) It may also be as subtle and impossible to spot as the man and woman who attend the open house that your company hosts, listen attentively, appear to be quite impressed by what they see during the guided tour and leave with a handful of brochures, just like everybody else who showed up.

Taken from ***Diplomats and Terrorists II***,

> *The difficult work of the professional intelligence and security forces can and should be augmented by the eyes and ears of the local (my word) community. There is an important role for these citizens (my word) in this vital information effort. Terrorists do not operate in vacuums. They must familiarize themselves with intended targets; they have to develop escape routes (my words–sometimes, but not always, for example, as in the case of the suicide bomber); they must obtain transport; place equipment in advance; plant explosive devices; acquire deceptive clothing or uniforms; and obtain documents. For some period of time they must leave their normal shadows and move into a community in order to plan or execute their activities. It is at this stage that alert and observant personnel could, and often do, sound the alarm based on some suspicious event, object or person they have observed while going about their daily affairs.*

At this point I think it will be useful to take a look at the terrorist attack planning cycle because it will help us to better understand what they need to do and why they need to do it. This will show us the vulnerabilities in the planning cycle that we can take advantage of. The cycle is a seven step process. Each step will have its own time line:

1. A target list is developed (can take years)
2. Initial surveillance is conducted on the targets (can take years)
3. Target selection takes place (can take years)
4. More surveillance is conducted on the target and operational planning and preparation begins (may take years)
5. The operational element moves into position (now we're talking hours and minutes)
6. The target arrives or they arrive at the target (usually minutes)
7. The attack occurs (over in seconds)

From this you will see that they become vulnerable when they "come out of the shadows" at steps 2 and 4. Here is where we can interrupt the cycle. If it is allowed to progress to steps 5-7 the odds heavily favor the attackers.

So what are we looking for? What should alert us that something is going on? If I can sum it up in a couple of phrases they would be "suspicious activity" and "suspicious attention." What someone is doing alerts you and/or they seem overly interested in what they are asking you or what they are looking at. Common sense tells you that this doesn't look right. It doesn't pass the smell test. Let's look at some recent examples.

- While this happened overseas the point still serves as a valid, if sad, example. Two Americans and a Brit are kidnapped from their apartment. All are subsequently beheaded. Prior to their abduction their security guards told them they were being watched. Then the guards quit showing up for work.
- A family boards a commercial flight and notices that a large group of males, who appear to be middle eastern, also board.

Once in flight they note there is a lot of eye contact and hand gesturing between the men. Some get up and go to the restroom with their carry-on bag that appears to be full when they head for the restroom and empty when they return. There's more but you get the idea. The official version was that this was a group of musicians. Well maybe. The point here is that the passengers noted what they considered to be highly suspicious activity and they reported it. They got it right. We'll come back to this one in a minute because it raises some other issues we need to discuss.

• There is reporting that suggests that Border Patrol agents are coming across increasing numbers of people they describe as OTM's (Other Than Mexicans) in the groups they encounter on our southwestern border. Some are identified as Arab speaking. Who are they? Why are they coming here? Where are they going? We know, for example, they have sometimes moved into Latin border communities in an attempt to hide themselves and their activities. Somebody somewhere is seeing these people and knows they are up to no good.

• Recently the Pakistanis arrested a senior Al-Qaeda official with a computer full of surveillance reports. The information was apparently determined to be several years old, (see the time lines above), possibly pre-9-11, and was gathered at a number of major U.S. financial institutions. The information was apparently quite detailed. And yet no one reported anything suspicious while it was being collected. No one noticed what was actually going on.

• We hear of sightings of individuals at dams, near nuclear facilities, VA hospitals, phone companies, military and government installations, bridges, tunnels, seaports and so forth taking pictures. This used to be a routine non-alerting activity but no longer.

The incident involving the family on the airplane raises the issue of racial profiling. Profiling can be a useful tool, in my opinion, but it is just that, a tool. Used as a stand-alone technique it can lead you down the wrong path with blinders on. For example, in this incident it might have been alerting but if nothing further had happened the men would have been unremarkable.

However, if we consider the actions of these men once the plane is in the air, then we have a whole different situation. The terrorists are certainly aware of this factor and they are actively recruiting from other cultures to give themselves a different look. They are supposedly using women more frequently for the same reason.

There has also been reporting that terrorists are experimenting with putting a group of people on a flight, each with a component of an explosive device. Once the plane is airborne, these pieces are assembled. This gives a whole new significance to passengers going to the restroom with full bags and returning to their seat with empty ones. To make matters worse, we know that the terrorists may do a dry run on a target to practice the drill prior to the big day, check for security reaction and response times, etc. This is why I suggest that you focus on "suspicious activity" and "suspicious attention," regardless of race or sex. They are more certain indicators that you should pay attention to.

We need to pay attention to what is going on around us and, if we think we are seeing something that needs to be checked out, we need to contact the authorities. *Who do you call?* Good question. For your information to do the most good it ultimately needs to end up at a Joint Terrorism Task Force which is run by the Federal Bureau of Investigation. They will probably have the best chance to make some sense out of what you report and its importance. In some cases, especially if you have a JTTF in your town or a nearby city, you may choose to contact them directly. Most, if not all, local law enforcement agencies will have someone you can talk to who will know how to contact the JTTF if you do not have one close to you. If you work for a large company and your concerns are caused by something that happens in the workplace then you will most likely take it to the corporate security office and they will deal with it. Regardless, **I cannot overemphasize the importance of getting your information to the authorities.** Secretary of Defense, Donald Rumsfeld has been quoted as saying, *It's not going to be a cruise missile or a bomber that's going to be the determining factor... It's going to be a scrap of information.* And you may be the one to supply it. Pay attention to what's going on around you. If it doesn't look right, report it.

I heard this during a recent interview with a wife and mother who lives in a high risk terrorist environment. The journalist asked her what precautions she took when she was outside of her home. *She replied, I open my eyes. I open my mind.* What a superb response and good advice for us all these days.

Chapter 14

The Personal Defense Handgun

"Is it possible to empty-hand defeat an opponent with a gun? Yes, of course it is. But in addition to skill, the martial artist must be very lucky. And the man with gun must be very stupid."
- Sekeichi Toguchi, Karate Grandmaster

Since you can't write a book on personal security these days without discussing handguns, probably the first question we need to ask is, "Are you ready for the responsibility that comes with owning a firearm for personal defense?" In addition to what you perceive as your level of risk, which we discussed in chapter one, there are other considerations such as your moral and ethical views on using deadly force, do you have small children in the home, are you fully committed to the serious responsibility involved in living with a loaded firearm on a daily basis, how frequently can you practice, and so on.

These handguns are excellent choices for concealed carry, personal defense: (clockwise from top right) The Heckler and Koch USP Compact, the Glock 23, the Glock 27, the SIG-Sauer P-225 and the Smith & Wesson 3913.

More food for thought. Most threatening situations are resolved without firearms. However, a good many potential problems are turned off by the mere display of a firearm. Hence the seriously flawed logic of thinking you will use a handgun only to scare away your attackers. If you need a handgun, you generally need it badly. If you are not prepared to use it, and your bluff fails . . . Handgun ownership is a big decision and many people who are very serious about their personal security choose not to own one.

If you decide that a firearm is a necessary part of your personal security plan then you need to obtain the best training you can afford. Schools such as Thunder Ranch, the Gunsite Training Academy, Defense Training International, Tactical Defense Institute, the Lethal Force Institute or the Blackwater Training Center will give you excellent training that will stand you in good stead both on the street and in the courtroom. Many of these schools will bring their training to you if you can't go to them. In addition, NRA programs, your local police and the training required to obtain your concealed carry permit are also training sources that you should take advantage of. Books and videos are training aids, but they are no substitute for the real thing. I strongly recommend the "Kelly McCann Video Series," available from Calibre Press, for their solid, proven content (P.O. Box 1307, Boulder, CO 80306, 303-443-7250).

SAFETY

No matter where you are (range, street, home) there are four basic safety rules that will always serve you well. However, simply reading them will not make them habitual. There is no substitute for hand's-on training to develop good safety habits and the necessary gun handling skills that are the mark of a responsible gun owner.

"Indexing" the trigger finger is a better idea than just extending the finger down the side of the frame. To index, the trigger finger is pointed inward and the touches the frame. In the event the shooting hand is involuntarily tightened, the finger will not "sling shot" back on to the trigger, as it is likely to do when the finger is merely kept straight.

1) ALL GUNS ARE ALWAYS LOADED

2) NEVER LET THE MUZZLE COVER ANYTHING YOU ARE NOT WILLING TO DESTROY

3) KEEP YOUR FINGER **OFF** THE TRIGGER UNTIL YOUR SIGHTS ARE **ON** THE TARGET

4) BE SURE OF YOUR TARGET

THE TOOLS

When Ed asked me to put together this section of our book I foolishly thought it would be a piece of cake. Frankly, a year later, knowing what I know now, if he approached me with the idea I'd run the other way. The hardest part has been identifying useful information that would fit our self-imposed simplicity requirement while leaving out lots of equally important and necessary information. This is why we keep repeating the importance of getting practical instruction from qualified professionals. Keep that in mind as you read through this. We're only hitting the high spots. We purposely left out comparisons, such as this grip vs. that grip or this gun vs. that gun so I want you to keep in mind that what I will talk to you about is just one way. It is not the only way. But it is the distillation of my many years of teaching rookie cops and legally armed citizens. Budget, time constraints and limited opportunities for refresher training required me to constantly search for simple effective techniques that would give my students the skills they needed. I am a charter member of the club that supports the old saying, "Advanced training is nothing more than the basic's mastered."

Handgun selection: The single biggest mistake that I have seen when someone selects a defensive handgun is that they pick either the largest or the smallest handgun they can find. While a full-size Colt 1911 or a Smith and Wesson model 29 .44 Magnum are certainly fine handguns, with a great deal of on-target power, they are also large handguns that many people will find cumbersome to keep with them at all times. The opposite ends of the spectrum are those small .22 and .25 caliber pistols that will fit in the palm of the hand. Yes, it is true such guns can be dropped in a pocket and forgotten. However, the primary reason for carrying a handgun is to stop a determined aggressor. The history of these handguns in actual combat has told us that without an extremely well-placed shot, they are not likely to do much more than irritate your attacker even more. And what are the chances of getting such a well-placed shot during a tense, fast-evolving situation? Like most things in life, selecting a personal handgun is a compromise. My advice is to obtain the most powerful handgun that you can shoot accurately and quickly and that you will always carry on your person. As Clint Smith has said many times, "Handguns are not supposed to be comfortable. They are supposed to be comforting!"

The handgun must fit you. When I select a pistol for myself, the first thing that I look at is whether or not I can reach the trigger properly. Through personal experience, I have discovered that the finger should rest on the trigger somewhere between the first tip pad and the first joint, depending on one's hand strength. In this position, the trigger finger should have enough strength to press the trigger smoothly to the rear without interrupting the alignment of the muzzle to the target...a very hard thing to do without continued practice! Placement of the trigger finger must correspond correctly with proper grip placement on the gun. To achieve a proper grip, the gun should sit in the hand in alignment with the forearm, as if the gun's barrel was an extension of the hand and fingers. Where the extended index finger would point, so would the gun's barrel. Once the gun is in this position, the trigger finger should engage the trigger as described above. If the finger cannot reach the trigger, the gun is too large. If there is too much finger on the trigger, then it is too small.

Grip feel is very individual, but I like the gun to fit in my hand like a solid handshake. The grip should be long enough for the pinky finger to get a solid purchase on the gun. Many people do not realize how important the pinky finger is when drawing and firing a handgun. The three lower fingers help control recoil, especially during rapid shooting. Not using the pinky finger reduces this control by one-third. So my guidelines for selecting the proper combat handgun (for you) are:

1) Proper full-length grip that allows for the whole hand to comfortably fit the gun
2) Proper trigger finger reach that permits the finger to contact the trigger using no more than the first joint of the finger while keeping a little gap between the gun's frame and the outstretched trigger finger

3) A smooth trigger, not necessarily light, but smooth so that no "glitches" can be felt as the trigger is pressed to the rear
4) Rust resistant finish
5) High visibility sights that can be seen quickly when needed but not so large that they snag on clothing during the draw
6) Caliber .38 Special/9 mm or larger
7) Semi-auto versus revolver is totally up to the end user.

Holsters: Selecting a holster can be a truly overwhelming experience due to the large number of styles available. As your skill and experience grows you may find that you end up with several holster types based on specific situational requirements you

may have, clothing styles and so on. Your first holster and the one that will probably best facilitate your learning process should be a good quality strong side belt holster. It should be accompanied by the appropriate magazine or speedloader pouches and a sturdy belt designed to fit the holster

The Alessi CQC (left) and the Milt Sparks "Roadrunner" are excellent examples of simple, but effective, concealed carry personal defense holsters.

slots or loops and those of the ammo pouches. (The strong side is your dominant or shooting hand side. The weak side is your support hand side). This is one of the easiest of holsters to conceal and one of the easiest for the human anatomy to work with without complicated motor movements. My recommendations for the strong side belt holster are as follows:

1) Dual slots/loops, the so-called "pancake" design or an inside-the-waistband style both of which hold the gun close to the body while keeping the grip stable and in one location
2) A holster which will stay open at the top after the gun is withdrawn so that it can be re-holstered without having to use the support hand to replace it or the gun's muzzle to "wiggle" it in place

3) Traditional thumb break or open top design
4) A holster which is designed to fit the exact gun that it is intended for.
5) Leather or Kydex. Kydex fit and speed of draw are certainly something to consider.

Multi-fit holsters should be avoided.

THE FIRING STROKE

Of all the defensive handgun shooting skills, I believe a good firing stroke to be the most important. It is a fight stopper. It is a technique which will deal with a broad spectrum of personal defense scenarios requiring a handgun to resolve. It is intended to allow you to quickly bring your weapon to bear on your assailant and to rapidly and accurately fire a two or three round burst at distances of 21' or less. It is important that you understand this may be all you have time to do. The firing stroke is composed of four parts. These are Stance, Grip, Front Sight and Trigger Action. The gun may already be in your hand (the Ready Position) or you have to produce it from the holster (the draw). I will walk you through the process starting with the pistol (empty, unloaded, no ammo) in your hand.

The "third eye" ready position is best described as keeping the muzzle pointed in the same direction as the eyes. If the gun is needed, it is pushed straight to the target making a quicker, more accurate shot more likely. Trying to bring the gun up on to the target is more likely to result in under or over travel when under stress.

The Ready Position: The Ready Position is exactly what the name implies. Something has alerted you to the fact that you may need your handgun. The best place to have it, when you need it, is in your hand, not your holster. The Ready Position that I teach, I call the

"Third Eye Position" because, with a little practice everywhere your eyes look, the gun "looks." John Benner, president and lead instructor at the Tactical Defense Institute in Ohio calls this position "chest ready." This insures that the gun is always between you and your assailant so you can get into action quickly. As you develop your gun handling skills you will note that almost everything you do with the handgun to keep it running (reloading, malfunction drills) places both of your hands in approximately this same position, reinforcing the "Continuous Motion Principle" which I will explain shortly. The handgun is in the center of the body somewhere between the navel and the chest, with the arms locked down at the side of the torso. The wrists are locked. The gun is six to eight inches away from the chest. From this position you also have good control of your sidearm should your assailant attempt to wrest it away from you. The gun can be fired quickly from this position at "Reactionary Gap" distances if you are forced to. This is the zero to six feet range at which a spontaneous attack is the most difficult to stop. If your weapon is in the holster, you will not be able to draw it in time. If you have the gun already in your hand but have to raise or swing it into a firing position you're wasting time you don't have. If all you have to do is start pulling the trigger you may have a chance. I have trained more than 3,000 people (police cadets, police officers and citizens) in the use of the Third Eye Ready Position. This technique has proven to be useful in numerous actual armed confrontations, several of which have been recorded on police cruiser video tapes. I think it can work for you too.

Over the years, many students have asked why I do not use the classic low ready position as popularized by the great Jeff Cooper, a man I greatly respect. It's not that low ready is a bad position—it's not—it's just that many people use it wrong! I have seen many shooters pointing their gun down at their feet due to fatigue and thinking they are in low ready—not good. To my way of thinking, if the gun is lowered more than 12-18 inches below the eye to target line, it should be brought back into the body, not lowered to the ground.

Many will say that the third eye is unsafe as it allows the shooter to "cover" things they are not willing to shoot. For those who have a problem with that, the third eye can still be used, however, the muzzle is depressed. The gun is now pointed in the same direction as it would be in a low ready, but it is more stable for movement.

Stance: Your feet are about shoulder width apart and the foot on your weak side is a comfortable (walking) distance in front of the foot on your strong side.

Grip: The gun is held in your firing hand, supported by the weak hand, trigger finger indexed on the side or frame of the handgun, in the Third Eye.

Indexing: The position of the trigger finger in the Ready Position, or when drawing and re-holstering the handgun, is very important. If your trigger finger is off the trigger but improperly positioned and you slip, you are shoved, you are startled, you can fire the weapon without intending to. Worse yet, under the influence of survival stress, you may not even be aware you fired it. I recommend that your trigger finger be indexed (placed on something it will remember, something it can feel) on the side of the weapon. In the case of a Glock pistol, it may be the serrated take down lever. On a revolver it may be a screw head.

Front Sight: I am a strong believer in the use of the front sight since it gives the shooter a reference point for shot placement. Especially for the person who cannot get out and practice as much as they'd like (I place myself in this category), the front sight is a very important "crutch" to aid the shooter in bullet placement. If the front sight stays in the shooter's field of vision the entire time the trigger is pressed to the rear, it only makes sense the shot will be accurate. And shot placement is everything when trying to stop a determined adversary with your handgun. Just hitting him will most likely not do the job. It's just not good enough to hit your attacker; it is important that you hit your attacker in a vital (upper torso) area of the body. This can be assured to a higher level by using the sights. As Dennis Tueller says, "If you don't have time to aim, you certainly don't have time to miss."

The "contrasting sight picture" consists of a front sight that can easily be seen through the rear sight, even during a tense, fast evolving situation. Shown here is a rear sight that has been widened with a file and all but the green tritium globes have been blacked out. The front sight has been kept a bright white color so that when the gun is quickly brought to eye level, as in an armed confrontation, the sight will interrupt the field of vision.

My experience, through both interviews with gunfight survivors as well as personal situations, is that the human eye can see the front sight quickly, but it needs help. The front sight must interrupt the field of vision as it is brought up between the eyes and the target. If the eyes have to seek out the front sight it will likely be of no value. A contrasting front sight is what I recommend and teach to my officers. As with most things, they taught it to me. In the revolver days, when big orange and red inserts started showing up in handgun front sights, I noted that the officers I debriefed after a shooting remembered seeing those colors. Those with plain black sights usually never remembered seeing the front sight at all. When the semi-auto pistol became popular, most came with either a three-dot or a bar-and-dot sight system. While such an arrangement is good for precision shooting, it is not nearly as fast for the eye to find, as is the contrasting sight. I have my officers black out the rear dots or bars with a felt tip pen. Even with their tritium sights, I have them black out the white ring around the globes on the rear sight.

This being said, let me now say EVERYBODY POINT SHOOTS! Before you throw this book down, let me explain. Getting the gun to the target from ready or holster is done by FEEL. In order to get a handgun to the target consistently, hand to gun contact and arm extension must be done the same way time after time. This is accomplished by recreating the same motor actions or feel. By doing so, the gun will come up in front of the eyes, to the target, the same way every time, regardless of body position. The eyes will only be used on the front sight in the last millisecond. The gun must be brought up in front of the face for the eyes to come into play. If this is not "point shooting," I don't know what is. The truth be known, if you can see the rear of your handgun between your eyes and the target, you will likely get a decent hit.

Trigger Action: The single biggest problem with shooting any firearm, but particularly a handgun, is separating the trigger finger from the rest of the hand. When you think about doing this, you will come to realize that it is a tall order. As we go through our daily routine, the fingers of our hand work in concert with one another the way they were designed to function. If you grab a door knob, pick up a pencil or grab the steering wheel of your car, you will notice that the fingers and thumb oppose one another, but work together as a team. Now, a handgun is placed into your hand and you are asked to press the trigger to the rear without using the other fingers which are to stay firmly in place?! It is not hard to understand why people "milk the grip," "slap the trigger" or "push the trigger." All of these are descriptions of being unable to separate the action of the trigger finger from that of the rest of the hand. The trigger finger needs to be able to move the trigger to the rear in a pressing action. This is not a "squeeze." Squeezing is, again, an action that is undertaken by all of the hand, such as squeezing a rubber ball.

From the Ready Position, you look at the spot on your assailant that you want your rounds to hit. You drive or punch your weapon toward the assailant. As soon as the front sight interrupts your field

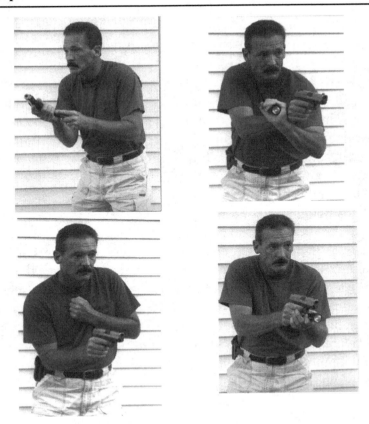

The third eye position is a big part of the "Continuous Motion Principle (CMP) philosophy of handgun training in that one position can be used for many things. This means that a lesser number of techniques need to be learned in order to master a particular skill. Note how the third eye position relates to using the flashlight (in multiple techniques), shooting with one hand in close quarters as well as speed loading the semi-automatic pistol. All of these functions are performed with the hands and arms in the same basic position.

of view between your eyes and your assailant, your finger will go onto the trigger. As your arms come to full extension, you press the trigger. As your speed develops this will become one fluid movement with the gun firing as soon as possible after your arms lock out in front of you. Using this technique, it is quite likely that a solid hit will be delivered to the target even if the front sight is lost during the stress of the moment. Using the contrasting front sight method during practice will establish proper body position for "muscle memory" shooting. As previously stated, this technique is also known as "point shooting."

The Draw: Now all we have to do is add the draw to what you have just learned. Once you draw the handgun you go into or through the "Third Eye" position. This is what I teach as the "Continuous Motion Principle" (CMP). CMP means all motions needed to complete an action flow into one another without having to throw a particular muscle group in reverse.

The draw should normally start with the hands in a common hand position which is normally in front of the body near the belt buckle. This is the normal position for our hands as we prepare to deploy our handgun. To make the draw one continuous smooth motion, your hand should move in a circular motion from the front of the body. This circular motion would be the same basic action as when you are drawing from under a jacket and must move the front edge of the coat out of the way to get to your sidearm.

Once your hand contacts the butt of the holstered handgun, the hand wrapping around the grip must be the same each and every time. To help you learn the proper hand placement, as your hand wraps around the butt of the gun in what you feel is the proper firing grip, index your trigger finger alongside the frame of the handgun (the holster will be covering the trigger finger index spot at this point). Your middle finger should be in contact with the bottom rear of the trigger guard. Press your middle finger against the trigger guard at this spot. This will cause a visible "dent" in the middle finger. This is the index point you need to achieve to get the same grip each time. If this finger location is achieved at the moment the hand impacts the trigger guard area, then the same grip will be assured, resulting in greater on-target speed.

The range commands I use during basic holster work may help you better visualize what the process is.

INDEX - Bring the hand up to the grip and sink the middle finger index point into the grip/trigger guard junction. Bringing the hand consistently to the holster is done by taking the shooting arm elbow straight to the rear. Wrap the three lower fingers solidly around the grip.

WRAP - Wrap the shooting hand around the gun, releasing the thumb break (if your holster has one) ON THE WAY to the proper shooting grip.

The gun needs to be drawn from the holster in a proper shooting grip each and every time. To accomplish this, get the unloaded gun in the shooting hand in the proper firing grip. Push the middle finger up into the junction of the trigger guard and grip.

This will leave a mark on the middle finger, which should be considered the draw stroke index point.

DRAW - Draw the handgun from the holster. Make sure the grip is in the desired location. Do not be concerned with speed.

When the draw begins, it is quite likely that the hands will be down at the side or in front of the body. Begin each practice draw from one of these normal body positions.

Bring the shooting hand to the holstered gun by taking the elbow straight to the rear and sink the middle finger index point into the trigger guard/grip junction.

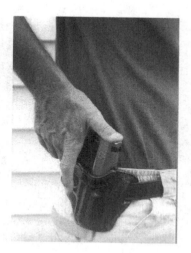

Once this index point is obtained, a proper shooting grip on the gun can be assured before the hand ever wraps around the gun. Note that at this point, only the three lower fingers are on the grip. As these three fingers curl around, the gun will start to come out of the holster.

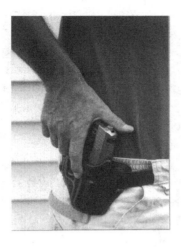

As the hand wraps around the gun to acquire the shooting grip, any thumb break retention devices will be released without making a separate motion.

The gun is lifted out of the holster enough to clear the holster mouth and then it is driven straight to the target.

The support hand comes over to join the shooting hand once the muzzle clears the body.

Now draw your handgun from the holster a few times and see where your hands come together as they drive to the target. WRAP your support hand around your shooting hand. You will not be surprised to discover that this occurs in the same general area as the Third Eye, thus making it a consistent action.

Once the gun is no longer needed, it should be replaced in the holster (finger off the trigger, properly indexed) from the rear to ensure that the gun will clear any retaining straps. A "thumb check" should always be performed on both semi-autos and revolvers to ensure the gun's hammer is not cocking when pushing the gun back into the holster. A thumb check is nothing more than placing the shooting hand thumb on the gun's hammer and holding it in place as you re-holster.

Note how the hands come together in the same basic position as the third eye ready position. This is another part of the CMP philosophy. One technique will work for multiple things!

Once you have developed your firing stroke to the point that you are both proficient and safe with it you'll want to begin practicing with live ammo.

Make sure you have eye and ear protection and a safe backstop. I would recommend sticking with simple drills of drawing from the holster or presenting the gun from the Ready and hitting paper plates at distances from three to seven yards. Many shooting schools place time limits on such drills, but I would be less concerned with how fast you are and more concerned with sharpening your skill. Work on performing the firing stroke correctly and I suspect that the speed will be there when the time comes. Be advised—speed comes from lack of unnecessary motion, not spastic muscle movement. The shortest road to incapacitating your assailant is to hit him in a vital spot. As the late Bill Jordan once said, "The history of gun fighting fails to record a single fatality resulting from a quick noise."

The shortest distance between two points is a straight line. Drive the gun to the target!

Once the hostilities have ceased, putting the gun back in the holster is done in reverse. Bring the gun back to third eye (CMP again!)

Making sure that the muzzle is never pointed at the body, bring the gun muzzle back past the holster and insert the muzzle of the gun into the holster mouth.

Shove the gun down into the holster, keeping the thumb on the slide making sure it does not go out of battery. This is called a "thumb check."

These are the other basic skills you will want to master.

1) How to reload your handgun rapidly. The gunfight stats indicate that reloads occur in very few police action or civilian shootings. Chances are you will solve or fail to solve the problem with what you have in your gun when the fight starts. But just in case . . .

2) How to clear pistol malfunctions quickly. If the malfunction cannot be cleared in a few seconds, RUN! Know to do this and instill it in your brain.
3) Practice shooting from standing, kneeling and while seated.
4) Be able to identify and practice firing from the types of cover found in the environment in which you live, travel and work.
5) Practice firing in low light and inconsistent light environments with and without a flashlight.

To draw from concealment, the same technique as described above is used. The only difference is removal of the covering garment. Do not make this garment removal process too complex. Remember, under stress, the hand will want to travel directly to the gun!

AMMO SELECTION

Like many law enforcement instructors, I collect data from actual shooting reports. I think this is as close as we can get to determining how well a bullet will do when it hits a body. But once again, these shooting reports can be considered nothing more than an indicator of performance. I have situations in my files where a particular bullet worked flawlessly on one occasion and then failed dramatically on another. This is the best justification I can think of for training to fire more than one round during a confrontation.

Two other data bases of actual shootings with which I am familiar are those of Massad Ayoob and Evan Marshall. Both of these men have been collecting data for well over a decade. Since much of their shooting data comes from different sources, they can be compared against each other to calibrate findings. To be included in Marshall's database, only one shot stops are considered. On the other hand, Ayoob includes multiple hit data in his base of information. Interestingly, even though they use different criteria for their databases, their results are similar. When rating the best loads in each caliber, their results are amazingly the same. Their findings are frequently published in various handgun magazines.

Actually, considering what was available when I began my law enforcement career, there is a wealth of excellent defensive handgun loads on the market today. All of the major ammo manufacturers such as Federal, Remington, Winchester, COR-BON, CCI-Speer, Black Hills, Hornady and so forth, offer ammunition specifically tailored to give maximum performance in a full range of handgun calibers.

I feel compelled to add, though, that bullet performance is secondary to shot placement in deadly force situations. The video, "Handgun Stopping Power," explains this point very clearly. It is available from Paladin Press, P.O. Box 1307, Boulder, Colorado 80306 (303-443-7250).

Chapter 15

Confrontation Tactics

Like the subject of handguns, entire books have been written on gunfight tactics. In this section we will take a simplified look at tactical basics for the lone individual. Armed encounters like the Hollywood Bank robbery, the NORCO Bank robbery, the FBI shootout in Miami and the Newhall Incident involving the California Highway Patrol are not the norm, even for police-involved shootings. These prolonged running gun battles are unusual in the history of gun fighting which clearly shows that most armed confrontations are quick, down-and-dirty affairs. Whether police, the military or citizens are involved, shootouts with handguns generally follow the "Rule of Three's." They take place at three yards (or less), are over in about three seconds (or less) and you will fire about three rounds.

My list of basic tactics, based on a detailed study of the subject during my 28 years as a street cop, is pretty short.

Learning how to recognize cover and to shoot around it is essential to any combat firearms training program.

1) Use cover to stop incoming fire from hitting you. Cover is any object that will stop bullets, not just hide your person. Don't underestimate conceal-ment. Not being seen goes a long way towards not being shot!

2) If cover is not available know how to remove yourself from incoming fire while returning fire at your assailant. This is better known as "shooting on the move."

3) Know how to control a suspect you are holding at gunpoint. This is a situation that is far more likely to occur than

shooting someone. This is known as "Threat Management" and the following are a few tips which will allow you to control a subject at gunpoint with a greater degree of safety:

a. Use forceful voice commands. BE FIRM. Let the suspect know that you mean business. An experienced criminal has a "sixth sense" as to whether or not a person will really use deadly force.

b. Get behind something as commands are given. EXPECT that the suspect will launch an attack against you. Put something between you and them. Act accordingly.

c. Place the suspect in a position that will make an attack difficult. The preferred position is lying on their stomach with their face away from your location, their arms and legs away from their body and the palms of the hands turned upward. If this is not feasible, have the suspect kneel with his legs crossed and his hands up in the air.

d. Never approach a suspect and try to search them or take them into custody. That is a job for the police. They are trained to do it. Let them! Stay in a guarded position and wait for their arrival.

e. Remember the 21'/360° rule. Criminals quite often work in "packs." Know what is going on behind you. "Check your 360!"

LOW LIGHT ENCOUNTERS

Human eyes do not work as efficiently in reduced-light settings as they do in full light. The retina, similar to the film in a camera, allows in light that interacts with light-sensitive cells called rods and cones. The cones, located in the central portion at the rear of the eye, work well in bright environments and enable

A quality flashlight, that gives enough light to see a threat even in the darkest of conditions, is essential. These are two excellent examples. On the left is the Laser Products model 6P while on the right is the Streamlight "Stinger."

color vision. Unfortunately, they do not function efficiently in poorly lit environments. Rods are located on the outer portions at the rear of the eye, and while they are not very efficient in bright light situations, they work well in low-light conditions. Also, since the rods are located on the outer portions of the retina, they are most effective for peripheral vision. This is why I teach my students to visually scan an area rather than focus on one particular point when trying to see in a low light environment.

The eye can adjust somewhat to low light conditions, but it may take anywhere from 20 to 40 minutes for full adjustments to occur. Think about your environment. When was the last time you had 20 to 40 minutes to allow your eyes to adjust to dim light before taking action? Have you ever had someone turn on the lights or shine a flashlight in your eyes once you have achieved night vision? That blinding effect could be very hazardous in an armed confrontation. You should also consider how consistent the light will be when you are out in reduced lighting conditions. People seldom work in a consistently dark environment. As a matter of fact, it is likely that the light will fluctuate, meaning that your eyes will never fully adjust to a single light or dark environment. Think of the last time you were walking down a street. There was probably street light that illuminated part of the area, while at the same time there were pockets of darkness behind a dumpster, around a corner or just beyond the reach of your flashlight's beam. Inconsistent light and shadows may interfere with your perception. You may be able to see an individual in poor light, but can you see him well enough to know if he is holding a weapon?

The survival smart thing to do is cast a light on a dimly lit situation using your flashlight. I recommend that your flashlight have a minimum of 60 lumens as well as a push-button on/off switch. My favorite lights are the model 6P and 6Z from Laser Products and the Stinger Rechargeable from Streamlight. These are lightweight, compact, quality flashlights.

A flashlight should be used in reduced-light environments to navigate, locate any threats and engage these threats if necessary. It may also be used to navigate a tactical retreat. But a light should only be on when you truly need it. Leaving the light on when you don't need it is greatly appreciated by the bad guy who may be lying in wait for you. Use your flashlight in short blips, then move. If your light does draw fire, you want to be standing in a different location. If you use your light to locate a suspect, they have, in turn, located you. Remember, to your advantage, you can temporarily blind a suspect by shining the light in his eyes, making him easier to overcome. At the Tactical Defense Institute, students are taught to "slash" with their flashlight across an opponent's face which is a very effective technique.

Firing weapons in a reduced light environment using a flashlight should be a required part of your training program. Many techniques have been developed over the years regarding the use of flashlights in conjunction with handguns. The methods which I demonstrate in the photos are the ones I have found to be the most effective during high-stress situations. I encourage you to try these techniques, pick your favorite, and use it consistently. Trying to master them all will only cause confusion during a high-stress event, creating a delayed response.

The Harries Technique places the shooting hand and the support hand back to back. Keep the support arm elbow as far down as possible to increase isometric tension.

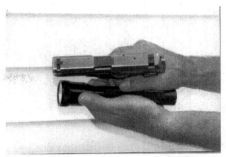

The Chapman Technique requires the flashlight to be held next to the gun with the thumb and index finger of the support hand wrapped around the flashlight with the thumb operating the activation switch. The three lower fingers are then wrapped around the shooting hand on the gun grip.

The Ayoob Technique has the shooting hand and flashlight hand held side by side. The two are not interlocked in any way, but the technique can be brought on target lightening fast. The beam will point upwards, but there will be enough light to identify the target.

The Rogers Technique is best employed with the Sure Fire 6Z Combat Light. Here the index and middle fingers of the support hand pull back on the flashlight body that in turn activates the rear mounted on/off button. The two bottom fingers can then be wrapped around the shooting handgrip. This technique is quickly becoming the choice of many armed professionals.

Sure Fire offers an excellent instructional CD which goes in depth into reduced light tactics. It is called "Choosing and Using the Tactical Flashlight" and it can be obtained from Sure Fire (18300 Mt. Baldy Circle, Fountain Valley, CA 92708, 800-828-8809)

OBSERVATIONAL SCANNING

Turning one's head does not mean that you truly see what is in front of you. In order to respond to any threat, you must see it first. Many people look, but do not see.

As part of any awareness program, you must teach yourself to scan the area around you in a consistent manner so that you will see a threat before it strikes. Close threats are of greater importance than distant threats, so it makes sense to look near before looking far when entering any new location.

For example, when most people enter a room, they look in the opposite corner first instead of on each side of the door they are entering—bad move. **Start scanning near to far** in a rhythmic, consistent manner from this day forward. It may just save your life, as it is likely that the closest threat is the most serious threat!

Chapter 16

Home Defense

For clarity's sake we distinguish home defense from home security. Home security is passive. We're talking about lighting, locks, alarms and such, which are way beyond the scope of this effort. Home defense is active. How do you deal with an armed intruder(s) in your home? We will deal with this in three segments, the gun in the home, the safe haven and leaving the safe haven. The previous chapter on confrontation tactics applies both on the street and in the home.

Keeping a Gun in the House

Without a doubt, the best way to keep a personal defense handgun is loaded and ready. If the gun is needed at a critical moment, all it will take to bring it into action is to draw, put the gun on target and press the trigger. What could be more simple?

But what if the gun is to be kept in the home and not on the person who is likely to use it. This is the big difference between a personal defense handgun and a home defense handgun. If children or other unauthorized gun handlers will never be in your home, then keeping a loaded handgun unattended will be just fine. But who lives in such a place? Guns are like a magnet for children and teenagers. For that matter, most of us have adult friends who are not "gun savvy." They have grown up watching their favorite heroes take care of the bad guys with a gun. Yes, it is certainly possible to train our children to respect guns, but what of their friends? Will your own child give in to peer pressure and let his or her buddies "play" with daddy or mommy's gun? Quite likely, in my personal experience.

For those of you who do not live in a "gun utopia" and must be concerned with potential undesirable gun handlers, the following guidelines are in order:

1) Keep your gun(s) locked up.
2) If keeping the gun locked up is not feasible (for most home defense situations it would not be), then consider keeping an easily manipulated trigger lock on the handgun. There are many different styles available and one is quite likely to meet your needs. Make it a model that is easy to open and does not require complex motor function to manipulate.
3) Consider keeping the gun unloaded, and next to a fully loaded speed loader or magazine. It only takes a few seconds to load the gun and bring it into action and it is not a threat until loaded.

Whatever you decide, do not keep the gun next to your bed or under your pillow. If you are suddenly awakened in the night, you will want to give yourself a few moments to wake up so that you do not mistakenly shoot your spouse or child who has gotten up to use the bathroom. Keeping a trigger lock on the gun or having to load the weapon first will give you the few moments needed to wake up and clear your head before taking action.

Additionally, if the suspect is on top of you when you wake up, it is not likely that you will have enough time to respond even if the gun is under your pillow. Lastly, a gun under the pillow is more likely to shoot YOU in the head than any home invader.

The Safe Haven

He was sitting in front of the TV, drinking a beer, munching potato chips and wondering what he was going to do for supper when he thought he heard a noise in the kitchen. He got up and poked his head around the corner of the door leading into the hallway. From the kitchen door, at the other end of the hallway, a strange face greeted him. He made all possible haste, as they say, to his safe haven, armed himself with a shotgun and called the police. When they arrived, the intruder was gone. He had apparently entered the apartment and left it through a tiny bathroom window which overlooked the apartment balcony. It was the only window in the apartment without bars. The apartment was on the eleventh floor of the building complex.

You may have also heard these referred to as safe rooms or core defensive areas. My message, in keeping with the theme of this book, is really simple. They work. Ideally, the safe haven is a fortified fighting position which will allow you to hold off the threat until the authorities arrive. I know of six cases in which safe havens were used. In every case the home owner and his family survived unscathed. Interestingly, while an exchange of gunfire may have started the incident, once the people occupied the safe haven there was no further shooting. Duration of these incidents was from 30 minutes to about six hours.

With the exception of the incident described above, all the safe havens had grills on the windows and a sturdy door with appropriate locks. Some had weapons. All had working telephones which were used to summon aid. Drinking water, several flashlights with fresh batteries, a trauma first aid kit, a fire extinguisher, diapers and formula if you have infants to take care of, and a spare set of house keys are some other items you might wish to have on hand.

Leaving the Safe Haven

The best thing to do in the event of a home invasion is to stay in your safe haven. Let the threat come to you. But what happens if you have children and they are not in the safe haven when the intrusion occurs? Being a parent of three children, I can tell you exactly what I will do! Leaving the safe haven is filled with dangers that can never be eliminated, but following sound tactics can reduce them:

1) Know your home. The big advantage that you have when working through your home is that you know where the obstacles are. Avoid them and allow your opponents to "go

bump in the night." You can use this advantage to identify their location and neutralize them, if necessary.

2) Have a preplanned route to the area that you need to secure. Practice this route in daylight and then in the light conditions in which you are likely to be operating if a real home invasion occurs. Remember how the eyes work in inconsistent light and plan accordingly. Practice with your home defense gun UNLOADED. Work the corners in a "slice the pie" fashion. Keep the muzzle of your handgun between you and the location you are checking "muzzle leads to danger."

3) Use visualization techniques to keep your home defense plan fresh. Sit back and visualize several likely scenarios in which you may have to leave the safe haven and secure another area. Work out contingency plans in your mind. This will reduce the lag time that might occur if your original plan falls apart.

4) Once you have reached your new location, IT becomes the safe haven. Do not try and remove your loved ones to another location. It is unlikely that they have practiced as you have for this incident, so they will not move with the same level of skill or stealth.

5) Make sure that your spouse is trained in the safe haven concept. If you must leave to defend another location in the home, your spouse will need to defend his or herself. This concept is much easier to execute than trying to take them with you as you work your route to another location. Trying to watch for an opponent in the dark and worry about what someone else is doing is almost impossible.

6) Scan from near to far as described in Chapter 15.

Final Thoughts

When I originally wrote these finals words in the first addition, our embassies in Nairobi, Kenya and Dar Es Salaam, Tanzania had just been attacked. I remember being glued to the television set trying to get as much information as possible, but much of the rest of the country took little notice of the event. After all, it took place in Africa and that is a long way away. Several of the TV experts talked about a terrorist group called Al Qaeda but this new group did not catch the attention of American citizens. Unfortunately, that has all changed since 9/11/01...the entire world has now heard of Osama Bin Laden and his group Al Qaeda.

Bin Laden picked these two embassies because they were considered "soft targets". According to my sources inside the U.S. State Department's Diplomatic Security Service, a soft target is one in which the embassy has minimal security precautions in and around it. This is in direct contradiction to a "hard target" which is an embassy that security is very high and attacking it would be difficult and would prove costly to the attackers. I guess you could say that all of America was a soft target prior to 9/11. All of this has changed since that time. America and its citizens have awoken to a new way of life. No longer will we get complacent and let our citizens be attacked and killed... or will we? As the years have gone by, have many of Americans forgotten the lessons of 9/11 in exchange for the inconveniences that heightened security will result in? From the whining and complaining that I hear whenever I travel by air, I would have to say that they have. I wonder if Americans will ever have the willingness to truly become hard targets. Only time will tell.

While our society may not be ready to "harden up", that does not means that you as an individual cannot. What this book intended to do was make you aware of how to be a hard target...to make it difficult to attack you and, if someone chooses to do so, make it very costly for them. If you look like prey, you will be preyed upon. Like Ed, I am a consummate people watcher. The next time you go to the local shopping mall, take a few moments to watch people as they cross the parking lot from their car to the store. Or better yet, as they go from the store to their car with an arm full of packages. Very few will take the time to look around in a 360 degree arc to see what is going on around them. Most will look down at the pavement, deep in their own thoughts, oblivious to what is transpiring around them. Think for a moment, if you were a predator, who would you pick? The person who is looking all around...who will see you approach from a great distance? Or the person who is totally "switched off" to what is going on just a few feet from their person? One is prey and one is not. Again, if you look like prey, you will be preyed upon.

It does not matter if this condition is called a "soft target" or "prey", being unprepared to defend yourself is unacceptable... especially in this post 9/11 world. You must be an active participant in your fight or you will not prevail... it is as simple as that. It is unlikely that the cavalry will ride over the hill to rescue you at the last moment. In my book HANDGUN COMBATIVES, I talk about the NESS Brothers. They are AwareNESS and WillingNESS and both are needed for you to prevail. They must always be with you...part of your person, your existence! Awareness means that you have decided that you can be a target and that you need to prevent it. Willingness means that you are willing to learn skills to prevail, not just survive, and to use them to finish the fight...no matter what the cost! Ingrain these concepts in your mind...use them to prevail. WE WANT YOU TO WIN! WE WANT YOU TO ALWAYS COME HOME TO YOUR LOVED ONES UNHARMED! That is why we wrote this book.

> *Somewhere right now, someone is preparing so when they meet you, they beat you. Train hard and stay on guard!*
>
> – Dennis Martin
> CQB Services, Liverpool, England

Index

OTHER TITLES OF INTEREST
FROM LOOSELEAF LAW PUBLICATIONS, INC.

Handgun Combatives
by Dave Spaulding

Use of Force
Expert Guidance for Decisive Force Response
by Brian A. Kinnaird

Deadly Force
*Constitutional Standards, Federal Policy Guidelines,
    and Officer Survival*
by John Michael Callahan, Jr.

Essential Guide to Handguns for Personal Defense and Protection
by Steven R. Rementer and Bruce M. Eimer, Ph.D.

The Retail Manager's Guide to Crime and Loss Prevention
Protecting Your Business from Theft, Fraud and Violence
by Liz Martinez

Identity Theft First Responder Manual for Criminal Justice Professionals – *Includes Free Victims' Assistance Guide*
by Judith M. Collins, Ph.D. and Sandra K. Hoffman, B.A.

Advanced Vehicle Stop Tactics
Skills for Today's Survival Conscious Officer
by Michael T. Rayburn

Advanced Patrol Tactics
Skills for Today's Street Cop
by Michael T. Rayburn

Path of the Warrior
  An Ethical Guide to Personal & Professional
  Development in the Field of Criminal Justice
  by Larry F. Jetmore

Powerful Pocket Guides - the Lou Savelli Series
  Gangs Across America and Their Symbols
  Identity Theft - Understanding and Investigation
  Guide for the War on Terror
  Basic Crime Scene Investigation

  (800) 647-5547   www.LooseleafLaw.com

PERSONAL SECURITY IS A WORKING BLEND OF AWARENESS, ATTITUDE AND TRAINING WHICH ALLOWS US TO CONFIDENTLY GO ABOUT THE DAILY BUSINESS OF LIVING.

*"**Ed Lovette** and **Dave Spaulding** have distilled over 50 years of hard-earned experience into 100 pages of street-proven wisdom. There's everything you need to know and not one word more."*

Marcus Wynne,
Trips Magazine

*"**Defensive Living**" addresses the human factors of self-protection. The lessons are not based on theory, but are the product of hard-won experience. **Ed Lovette** and **Dave Spaulding** are highly respected instructors/writers in the tactical "community" and both can "walk their talk."*

Dennis Martin,
CQB Services
International Training Activity

*"Manuals on the use of firearms and other fighting skills are somewhat commonplace. Authors **Lovette** and **Spaulding**, however, draw on their many years of experience and present a more encompassing strategy for staying safe. "**Defensive Living**" should be required for anyone concerned about their personal safety in an increasingly hostile world."*

Lt. Mike Boyle
Contributing Editor
Guns & Weapons for Law Enforcement